EVERY SOBER DAY IS A MIRACLE

EDITED BY
JOHN R. CHEYDLEUR, Ph.D.
WITH
ED FORSTER

CREST BOOKS

Copyright © 2010 by The Salvation Army

Published by Crest Books
The Salvation Army
National Headquarters
615 Slaters Lane
Alexandria, VA 22313
Phone: 703/684-5523
Fax: 703/302-8617

Major Ed Forster, Editor-in-Chief
    and National Literary Secretary
Judith Brown, Crest Books Coordinator
Lisa Jones, Cover Design

Available from The Salvation Army
Supplies and Purchasing Departments
    Des Plaines, IL – (847) 937-8896
    West Nyack, NY – (888) 488-4882
    Atlanta, GA – (800) 786-7372
    Long Beach, CA – (847) 937-8896

Printed in the United States of America

Library of Congress Control No: 2010921499

ISBN: 978-0-9792266-8-7

*This book
is dedicated
to all the children
of the men and women
whose lives
have been reclaimed
from the doorstep
of hell itself.*

"I am not proud to say
that I sunk as low as
you can get. I lived
under a bridge, ate out
of the garbage, and
all other things. . . .
"But now I am a new man
in Christ, and I have a
future—a good future—
waiting for me!"

Anonymous delegate
Ladore Holiness Retreat

CONTENTS

Foreword xi
Introduction xv
About Our Contributors xvii
If Today Is Your First Day of Sobriety xix

I. STARTING AT THE TOP
Golf Pro Turned Barroom Brawler 3
All Good Things Ended 6
My Ship Ran Aground 8
Perfect Childhood Ends in Jail 10
I Lost My Childhood Sweetheart 13
Why I Quit the Coast Guard 16
Small-Town Kid Becomes Drugstore Bandit . . 18
Good Jewish Boy Goes to Jail 21
Honor Student Beaten by Her Dope
    Dealer 23

II. BEGINNING AT THE BOTTOM
Doing Drugs with Mom 27
Boy Arsonist 29
Fourteen Years of Hard Time 32
My Gods Were Demons 34
Growing Up in the Gutter 36
Dad Tied Me to a Radiator 38
Drunk Father, Drunk Son 41
Molested by My Uncle 43
A Young Old Man 45
Sudden Death 47

III. THE LOW ROAD OF ADDICTION

Good Girl Gone Bad 51
Play Now, Pay Later 55
My Dad Taught Me to Drink 58
Violent Childhood, Violent Marriage 60
Alcohol Was My Mistress 62
Runaway 64
The Nightmare Every Parent Fears 66
Lived to Get High 68
B. A. in Boozology 70
Trapped in a Compactor! 72

IV. ATTEMPTING RECOVERY WITHOUT JESUS CHRIST

Pharmacist Junkie 79
Had a Good Job, But Couldn't Keep It 82
Third-Grade Drunk 84
No Luck without Jesus 86
Flunked out of Forty Detoxes 88
Always Something Missing 91
Street-Gang Member 93
Marriage Was Not the Cure 95
From Street Kid to Street Bum 97
I Thought God Wanted Me to Be an
   Alcoholic 99

V. DISCOVERING THE ARC

From Addict to Editor 105
The ARC in My Neighborhood 107
When the Fog Lifted 109
"Useless" 111

Broke a Window to Find Jesus 114
Found a Balanced Life 116
"Cinderella" 118
I Asked the Court to Let Me Quit the ARC . . 120
Love in Old San Juan 122
Graduates Always Welcome 124

VI. THEY FOUND JESUS THE SAVIOR
Cocaine Roller Coaster 129
Rescued from Amphetamines 131
I Heard Jesus Speak 133
AWOL in Omaha 135
I Found Jesus at the V. A. 138
Jesus Gave Me Self-Respect 140
Time Bomb! 142
From Failure to Faith 146
No Love Here 148
Became a Real Mom When I Found Jesus . . 150

VII. ONE DAY AT A TIME
I Try to Be Kind 155
I Used to Live under the 10th Street
    Bridge 157
Slow and Steady Wins the Race 160
Haven't Had a Drink Today 162
God Is Healing Me 164
Orphan-Alcoholic-Bible Teacher 166
Peace Is Better than Control 168
Don't Take Jesus for Granted 170
Not Afraid to Succeed 172
My Wife Didn't Have to Take Me Back 175

VIII. THE POWER OF FAITH

Welcome to America? 181
At Peace with Myself 184
I Opened My Heart to God 186
Given the Last Rites 188
Learning the Basics 190
God Replaced That Lonely Feeling 192
A Contented and Productive Life 194
Ambassador for Christ 196
Policeman, Priest, or Wise Guy? 199
Jesus Is the Source 202

IX. THE FAMILY OF GOD

Channel of Love 207
Salvation Soldier 210
Back in the Family of God 213
Touched by the Holy Spirit 215
Real Friends and Family 217
A New Sense of Family 220
I Left the Circus and Joined the Salvation
    Army 222
Miracles Still Happening 225
The Right Place 227
A Father's Letter 230

X. THERE IS A FUTURE

Sixteen Years of Sobriety 237
Married and Working Full-Time 239
Ticket to a Successful Future 241
Education, Career, and Marriage 243
Sober and Solid 245

Today I Have a Wonderful Family 247
Pleasure Out of Failure 250
I Found Out How to Live 254
State-Certified Alcohol- and Drug-Abuse
    Counselor 256
Disc Jockey for Jesus 259
My Own Story 263

Special Thanks 265

FOREWORD

John Cheydleur and Ed Forster have created a valuable and inspiring book for people recovering from alcohol and drug addiction, or those just beginning to suspect that they may have a problem.

Each of the 99 segments has a brief, true story of an alcoholic's or addict's personal background, the beginning and course of his or her addiction, and the crisis that led to treatment at one of the 119 Salvation Army Adult Rehabilitation Centers across America. These stories contain dramatic and sometimes stark revelations of such things as loneliness; dishonesty; molestation by family members; beatings; other kinds of abuse; brawling; going to jail; unfaithfulness; losing family; losing social standing, jobs, and possessions; and the miracles of finding recovery, hope, and a relationship with God in a community of caring people. It would be difficult for an alcoholic or addict not to find places to identify with in this straightforward and honest book.

Each story is followed by a brief, biblically based meditation and a prayer, so the book makes an excellent daily devotional tool for people on the road to recovery. Having a real-life story of authentic change to think about every day and a chance to meditate and pray about one's own life and recovery can really be helpful in establishing the habits of hope.

The editors have divided the ninety-nine segments into ten sections, each section containing nine stories about people coming into recovery from different places in life (e.g., *Starting at the Top, Beginning at the Bottom, The Low Road Of Addiction*); different ways of trying to get sober (e.g., *Attempting Recovery without Jesus Christ, Discovering the ARC, They Found Jesus the Savior*); valuable principles and tools of recovery (e.g., *One Day at a Time, The Power of Faith, The Family Of God*); and finally a section pointing toward the future entitled *There Is a Future*.

After reading the ninety-nine stories, one each day, the reader is offered a unique opportunity: There is space (and guidance for) the reader to write *his or her own story—in the book itself*, as the 100th segment. This can be a powerful way for the recovering person to identify with the community of those farther along in recovery and motivate him or her to continue with them in a life of sobriety and spirituality.

I think The Salvation Army ARC program is one of the most remarkable efforts I know. One of the unusual aspects of this largest adult rehabilitation program in the world (about 13,000 beds in the United States and Canada) is that, besides being unknown by many in the professional-treatment-center world, the spiritual component of the Salvation Army program is unashamedly Christian, while clearly promoting twelve-step principles and groups. Further, there is an extended supervised-living and work-therapy program for helping newly recovering people to absorb healthy living and working habits and become successful long-term providers for themselves in the working world. All of this is provided at no cost to most of the participants.

I hope this book will help thousands of people to find healing from the pain, frustration, and losses caused by their addictions, and a new life of hope and happiness.

J. Keith Miller
Author of *A Hunger for Healing* and
The Taste of New Wine
Austin, Texas

INTRODUCTION

An old, weather-beaten man sits on a dirty curb in a lonely city. A child-woman cries as she walks the early-morning streets, hunched over to protect herself from the ice-tinged wind. A handsome but worried-looking young man poses on a street corner again tonight—equally afraid of the police and of the man to whom he will sell his body for drugs.

Their public tragedies begin with private misery: A chubby eight-year-old boy is sent every morning to school with beer in his lunch-box thermos. A bright-eyed girl with pigtails is raped by her uncle at age eleven. A straight-A college student is introduced to drugs at his twenty-first birthday party.

Then, a door of hope opens at one of the 119 Salvation Army Adult Rehabilitation Centers in the U.S.A. It could be at the former auto warehouse in a major eastern metropolis, or small new brick building tucked almost invisibly along a side street in a mid western town, or a sunny stucco estate in rural California, or a block-long multiservice center in Texas. . . .

And Jesus reaches down, transforming another human being from misery to manhood, from despair to womanhood, from the streets to a sober new life.

These successful ARC graduates become cooks

and stockbrokers, moms and dads, car-wash attendants and radio announcers, preachers and auto salesmen; in fact, they are now represented by thousands in every walk of life.

These are some of their stories, the true stories of the men and women of The Salvation Army Adult Rehabilitation Centers—for whom *Every Sober Day Is a Miracle!*

ABOUT OUR CONTRIBUTORS

Each of the fascinating stories in *Every Sober Day Is a Miracle!* is true.

The people, events, and places are true.

Every contributor (except two) has given permission for her/his true first name to be used, and many were willing for their full names to be printed, although the editors decided to maintain a measure of anonymity by using first names only.

But their lives are not static. By the time you read this book, many of our contributors will have become even more stable in their recovery, some may have relapsed, and still others will have become deeply involved in helping others on the way up.

As Robert Schuller puts it: "Success is never certain, but failure is never final."

Please pray for each of our contributors by name, for they each have much life still to live, either as sad people, defeated by their addictions, or as sober, happy, victorious Christians!

John R. Cheydleur, Ph.D.
Ed Forster
Editors

If Today Is Your First Day of Sobriety

Start at the beginning of this book.

If you want to preview our whole book quickly, read each of the section introductions and the first story in each section, but don't read the other stories and meditations and prayers. Not yet.

Then, go back to the beginning. Read one story and one meditation, and pray one prayer each day for ninety-nine days.

You may want to look up each of the Scripture references or add your own original prayers.

Then, on the 100th day, write out your own personal story. You can also choose your favorite Bible verses and write out a prayer to go with your story.

Put them in the place provided in the back of this book.

Then you will have completed the book, and you will have completed 100 days of sobriety, one day at a time, one story at a time.

Congratulations in advance from all of us !

*The Men and Women Graduates of the
Adult Rehabilitation Centers*

ONE

STARTING AT THE TOP

It is a common mistake to think that addiction, whether to alcohol or to other drugs, cannot affect those who come from a "good home" or had a "good upbringing."

But addiction is an equal-opportunity destroyer. It can affect anyone—of any race, social status, or positive family background. When the chemical takes over, all people are destroyed equally. The chemical becomes god. Everything and everyone else becomes unimportant.

But there is hope! Brian's story is proof of the power of addiction and of the possibility of recovery. . . .

GOLF PRO TURNED
BARROOM BRAWLER

*I*t was a wonderful life. Brian was athletic and strong. Given the choice to play tennis or golf professionally, he chose golf.

"My problems with addictions began while I was the golf pro at a country club in Bridgeport. It was the beginning of a bad journey.

"The only alcoholic I had ever known was my grandfather. My father would always get upset when my grandfather came to our house for the holidays. He knew my grandfather would make a spectacle of himself, but I loved the man.

"We would always have to pull his car out of the driveway for him because he was too drunk. On reflection, my grandfather was a very bitter person. How could I have known that years later, I'd be just like him?

"I was always very possessive. Though I didn't know what made me that way, I acted it out by being abusive—physically and mentally. I liked my beer, til I got to the point of drinking bourbon and vodka.

"After four years as a golf pro, I had to give it up. Financially, I was set because my father owned a glass company. He paid me $15.00 an hour, with an expense account, too. My father, the great enabler, gave me anything I asked for. This fueled my addiction.

"My arrest record began when I was nineteen. It was a family fight—brothers against brothers and cousins against cousins. It was a Code 50—all police within hearing distance had to respond. During the melee, I broke a police-car window and a policemen's arm. I got three years' probation and four weekends in jail.

"I couldn't deal with the probation, so I took off for South Carolina with my wife-to-be, Jill, but we didn't stay long. When we came back from the South, I went back to the judge, and he gave me another three years' probation, which I followed through with. I must admit, I drank the whole time I was on probation—they never tested me.

"Most of my thirty-six arrests were for barroom fights. I was put in jail five times. My marriage to Jill failed after we had four children together. Then the death of a cousin in a tragic car accident pushed me deeper into my addiction.

"I drank every day at a bar in Syracuse. A barmaid introduced me to cocaine with the simple words, 'Here, try this.'

"After this, the lying, stealing, and thievery increased steadily. My continued drug abuse nearly destroyed me.

"When I came to the ARC, I was in very

bad shape physically and mentally. The ARC helped me and lifted me up.

I was the golf pro at a country club in Bridgeport.

"I went to an ARC retreat in 1992 and accepted Christ as my Savior. I felt wonderful again! With AA and a Higher Power, I thought I had all the answers. I decided I was ready to be on my own again, so I left the ARC and went back to my dad's glass company. When I got my first paycheck, I got drunk and high again. I was right back where I had started.

"During the next three months I went to two AA meetings a day. I got a sponsor, a home group, and I prayed every day. I now realize that I have to work daily on my sobriety. Each day, I talk to the Lord, my counselors, and I attend meetings. I am also an employee at The Salvation Army.

"The thing we all need to remember is that we are all God's children. I hope that somewhere someone will realize, through my story, that with God there is always a way."

MEDITATION: *We have a covenant with our God, who wants to multiply us* (Gen. 17:2). *God's promises are for us and our children* (Gen. 17:7). *God wants to bless us with prosperity and security* (Gen. 17:8).

PRAYER: *Even when I have lost everything, Lord, I will trust You and believe that You want the best for my life.*

ALL GOOD THINGS ENDED

*I*t was expected that Mary Jane would always be perfect. Those high expectations set her up for failure. She learned when she was very young that life would go smoothly if she pleased her parents. She also learned not to let anyone know how she felt or what she felt. It seemed to her that her feelings weren't important.

"I grew up in a Catholic family, and my father was very strict. I remember great pressures as a child and as a teenager in all areas of my life.

"As a result of my responses to life, I've had several problems. My alcoholism was the only way I took to cope with life's problems. I neglected myself because I felt I always had to make everyone else happy.

> **Life would go smoothly if I pleased my parents.**

"Since coming to the ARC over a year ago, I've been relearning how to live. I've learned that God is the only answer to my problem with addiction.

"I turn my will over to Him at the beginning of each new day. He guides me through the day. He always lets me know when I am trying to take my own will back. Faith and conviction have been the keys to my recovery.

"I am a live-in employee at the Army now. I've learned to trust others. Finally, I am able share with someone what's going on inside of me.

"It is only by the grace of God that I am here. It is a joy to be part of a family at the ARC that truly cares for me."

MEDITATION: *Nothing is too hard for our God* (Gen. 18:10-12). *The only thing between us and our miracle is time* (Gen. 18:14). *Our God fulfills His promises to us* (Gen. 21:2).

PRAYER: *Your ways are beyond my understanding, Lord. I will believe that You know more than I do.*

MY SHIP
RAN AGROUND

*I*f having a happy childhood could solve all of life's problems, Gary would never have become addicted. He had a good relationship with his father and mother, as well as with his brother and sister. They were a close family that did things together. Gary grew up in a middle-class neighborhood and attended private school.

When the time came for higher education, his parents sent him to college. Gary has fond memories of his growing up years and remarks, "I feel that I was very fortunate in my upbringing and I wouldn't change a thing."

After college his problems began. He went to work for his father in the boat business. After ten years, his father retired. For two more years Gary ran the business in a New York City borough and then decided to relocate the business to New England.

The economy turned bad. The boat business went bust, and Gary declared bankruptcy.

"I blamed my heavy drinking on my circumstances, but I was already an alcoholic," admits Gary.

He gradually went from being a materially successful man with a hidden drinking problem to a struggling restaurant manager whose disease was obvious and out of control. "My life became more unmanageable and my family became a shambles.

"Through the help I got at The Salvation Army and the AA meetings, I found a reason to keep going on," he says. "It was a long, hard process. Many times I wanted to quit. I felt that being reunited with God and with my family gave me hope to make it. I know I still have a long way to go."

I feel that I was very fortunate in my upbringing.

Gary lives in a halfway house now and commutes to work every day.

He says, "I like my job, and I feel that this is where I should be right now in my life."

MEDITATION: *When we do things our own way, it doesn't work out, but when we do what God tells us to do, it works* (Exod. 2:11-12; 4:28-31).

PRAYER: *Lord, teach me Your ways. Tell me what to do today, and I will do it.*

PERFECT
CHILDHOOD
ENDS IN JAIL

*M*y life as a child could have been considered perfect in the elements that are supposed to make for a happy individual, as well as for a healthy, contributing member of society.

Jerry had loving parents, two of them, who were firm but fair. He also enjoyed a country life and a good country-school education. Childhood in the country was low key and nurturing.

However, when he moved to Cozad, Nebraska, his brothers and sisters had left home, and friends and neighbors were few and far between. Jerry spent many long hours alone.

Jerry was still very much a loner when he graduated from high school. After high school he went to technical school in Hastings, about which he says, "About the only thing I really learned at tech school was how to drink, get drunk, and go on getting in trouble with my new so-called friends."

Jerry's need to drink in order to cope with his loneliness followed him to his only real job. After fifteen years with the company it went bankrupt, and Jerry was jobless.

He began to blame God more and more for his difficulties: "Drinking encompassed more and more of my life, and I became increasingly isolated and hopeless. The bottom finally fell out, and I lost even my home. My sister tried to help by letting me move to Omaha with her, but matters continued to deteriorate until I was homeless again and was arrested for something I didn't do."

My life as a child could have been considered perfect.

After a long stint in jail and an extended battle with the legal system, Jerry was finally released from jail, but he was homeless again. He had to go somewhere, and that somewhere turned out to be The Salvation Army ARC.

"The Salvation Army ARC was not what I expected at all! I came in expecting to find a human warehouse for filing away 'useless' people. It proved to be a place that helped people in need work on problem areas while keeping themselves drug and alcohol free.

"I have had trouble keeping a job over the last several years, so the work-therapy program is essential in helping me work out personality defects and shortcomings I have."

Jerry found that the religious services and other

religious programs were a lot harder for him to accept than the work therapy, but he says, "The AA meetings that I was required to attend during the ninety-day program helped me remember the reasons I need to stay sober. I am and always will be vulnerable to alcohol and other addicted behaviors, but, with the help of God, it did help me over the first difficult hurdles."

"Someday soon, with Divine guidance, I can find the courage to leave the ARC and start over again."

MEDITATION: *Our God lifts us up to Himself and asks us to obey His voice* (Exod. 19:4-5).

PRAYER: *I don't know how to worship You, Lord, but I know I will need You. Help me.*

I LOST MY CHILDHOOD SWEETHEART

*F*rank's love grew like a tree in Brooklyn. He says, "I met my wife in Sunday school, where I was also an altar boy and a member of the choir.

"We both grew up in a middle-class section of the borough in a relatively quiet atmosphere. My mother was active in the Lutheran church, although my father seldom attended.

"During the early '60s, I served as a Chaplain's Assistant in the military. After getting out of the service, I went into my wife's family bakery business. I became active in the Baking Industry Association, eventually serving as its president during the early '80s.

"I took over the family bakery business in 1977, and life ran fairly smoothly until 1979, when my brother-in-law developed cancer. After three years of devastating suffering, he died . . . he died in 1982, on my daughter's twenty-first birthday.

"My mother died soon afterward, the result of several strokes. Life became a strain. I was constantly at the bakery or doing bakery-association work, and alcohol was a big part of the association. With association meetings two or three times a week, I began to neglect my family. There was a lot of dining out and plenty of cocktails.

"My wife and I started to drift apart. She was into church activities—I was into the bakery business and alcohol. At the end of 1983, we separated. Three years later, after twenty-four years of marriage, we divorced. It was a shock to all of our friends.

"I signed the business over to my wife and daughters. Then I went to work for a friend from the association. Things were fairly normal, but alcohol was becoming a bigger part of the picture.

"God and church were always secondary, because I worked on Sunday and "couldn't" attend services.

"By the end of 1990, alcohol finally overtook me. I signed myself into Brunswick Hospital for a twenty-eight-day program. They told me my alcoholism, as serious as it was, was not my primary problem. They were worried about my mental state—I was suicidal.

I met my wife in Sunday school, where I was also an altar boy.

"Six months after my release from the hospital, I went to The Salvation Army ARC program. I finally came to realize that God and prayer, not alcohol, were the answers to my problem."

God had been knocking on

the door of Frank's life for a long time. He says, "I finally decided to open my life to Him." Frank's first work assignment at the ARC was in the sorting room. After his graduation from the program, Frank accepted a paid position with The Salvation Army in the bric-a-brac department.

Frank joined The Salvation Army Church as an Adherent in December of 1991.

Today, he says, "I have a beautiful room in a new building, good friends, and a chance for a new life."

MEDITATION: *We should offer God our best just as He gave us His best in the shed blood of Jesus Christ* (Lev. 1:2-3; 17:11); (John 3:16).

PRAYER: *Lord, I want to give You my best, but I'm afraid. Help me to know how much You love me.*

WHY I QUIT
THE COAST GUARD

*S*cott's story could have come right out of *Father Knows Best*. He says, "I had a pretty normal childhood. I grew up in a good neighborhood in a small town. I pretty much stayed out of trouble until I was in my late teens. My family had no real troubles that I remember; we had a pretty happy life."

However, at age 16, Scott started to drink and drug. He says, "Seemed like I got into trouble as soon as I started drinking. Nothing major, but I didn't get along with my family like I used to. I had a couple of scrapes with the police. I joined the Coast Guard when I was eighteen, and my drinking and drugging really escalated. Everyone who knew me knew I had a problem. I stayed in the service for four years, but I left because I wanted to drink more than I wanted to stay in."

After leaving the Coast Guard, Scott bounced around from job to job, although he did manage to work pretty steadily. Then, in 1986, his mother died.

Scott says, "It seemed like something inside of me died too. All I wanted to do was drink and drug and forget about life. I managed to do this for the next six years."

Scott tried several recovery programs but says that his real recovery did not begin until he came to the Worcester ARC. "I had been to programs before, but I always went for someone or something else, never for myself. I came here to Worcester for me and me only, and it was here that I began to find God. I had never been very religious, although in times of trouble I would always call on God. Here I began to see that God would help me in my recovery, and He has."

I grew up in a good neighborhood in a small town.

Scott has been clean and sober for ten months, and he says, "I know I didn't do it on my own."

At the time Scott sent us his story, he had just been hired to work in one of the Worcester Salvation Army stores. He says, "My continued sobriety is a huge success. I believe that things will only keep getting better."

MEDITATION: *We are not the people of the past* (Num. 13:28). *We are the men and women of the future* (Num. 13:30). *Our God does the impossible* (Num. 14:8).

PRAYER: *In You, Lord, all things are possible. I believe. Help my unbelief.*

SMALL-TOWN KID BECOMES DRUGSTORE BANDIT

Michael was born and raised in a small town in New Jersey close to the George Washington Bridge. He came from a basically nonalcoholic family. He says, "I was an average student in school and had a pretty normal childhood, experimenting with girls, sports, and music." He went to a well-known trade school in New Jersey and obtained his certificate in commercial baking, but his secret was that he had started smoking marijuana at age thirteen, and alcohol was increasingly invading his life.

Michael describes himself as "a follower, who did what everyone else was doing to be accepted. By the time I was eighteen, I was drinking just about every day. I bought my first and last car about this time. I was drinking and driving with a friend one night and I drove into an oil truck! My car was wrecked and we were lucky!"

At twenty-one, Michael became involved with two men who tried to rob a liquor store. There were no weapons and no one was hurt, but Michael was arrested and spent thirteen months in prison before being released.

"I also had problems with relationships and family problems from my drinking. I hit my bottom when I was twenty-nine. I was drinking morning, noon, and night. I lost my job and, finally, my apartment. I was stealing to get alcohol. I also had massive seizures and almost bit off my tongue. I wanted to kill myself."

Michael's brother-in-law played a major part in his recovery. When Michael was at the depth of his addiction, his brother-in-law tried to help him with a prayer to Jesus Christ. Michael reports, "We said the sinner's prayer together and the next day I was in a detox unit. Since that first day of my recovery, I truly felt the love that Jesus Christ has for me, and I've worked on my relationship with Him daily. I have come to know Him as my personal Savior, Friend, and Teacher. I believe that it is only through Him that I am alive, sober, and who I am today."

After graduating from the ARC program, Michael became an employee and kitchen supervisor at The Salvation Army. He says, "I am learning more about my abilities in the field of cooking and baking, and accepting the responsibilities of my job. I also have the opportunity to feed some of the homeless people in the area and

I was an average student in school and had a pretty normal childhood.

19

stay as active as possible with the fellowship here, all of which encourages my spiritual growth."

Mike concludes his story: "I am learning more about myself and how to live a sober life. Each day begins with new challenges and new blessings, and for this I am grateful."

MEDITATION: *We follow God fully, and He prospers us finally* (Num. 14:24). *We pray and listen to what God tells us to do* (Num. 20:6-8).

PRAYER: *Heal me of the sin of impatience, Lord. Let me do just what You tell me to do without pride or anger.*

GOOD JEWISH BOY
GOES TO JAIL

Steve was born and raised in a middle-class Jewish home in New York. As a boy, he had some problems with running away from home.

His parents wanted him to go for psychiatric treatment, but he refused. Instead, he put his energies into sports, and he played football in high school.

In the beginning, I only drank on weekends.

"When I was eighteen," he says, "I started drinking. It was mostly beer at first, but then I went to scotch. In the beginning, I only drank on weekends. Later, I began to drink more heavily and more often.

"I started smoking marijuana, and eventually I got into Valium and other pills. I left New York and went to California.

"While I was in California, I got desperate for money to do drugs. I attempted two robberies, got caught, and was sent to jail for two years.

"I came back to New York in 1983, still heavily into drugs. In February of 1984, I came to The Salvation Army ARC.

"My Christian conversion occurred that year at an Army congress. When I went to the altar to accept Christ, I got help in being a Christian from several people.

"I became an Adherent in The Salvation Army Church, and later a Soldier of The Salvation Army. Two years ago, I became an employee of The Salvation Army. Today, I work as a dispatcher.

"After a relapse, I went back to the ARC and really turned my life around, with God's strong guidance showing me the way.

MEDITATION: *We love God with our whole heart and soul. We love our neighbors as ourselves* (Matt. 22:34-40); (Deut. 6:4); (Lev. 19:18) .

PRAYER: *Lord, it is hard for me to love, but it is even harder to be torn up by hate. Teach me how to forgive, both myself and others.*

HONOR STUDENT
BEATEN BY HER
DOPE DEALER

*D*y-Ann got straight A's. She was at the top of her class. Her parents were always there for her, but her father was verbally abusive.

She says, "I was a lonely child. Being on the honor roll was great, but I was lonely for friends. In my attempt to fit, in I got involved with the wrong group. Soon I was taking pills, smoking marijuana, and letting peer pressure suck me into a terrible nightmare."

> **Being on the honor roll was great, but I was lonely for friends.**

In addition to the drugs, Dy-Ann says she was, "Into lying, stealing, and cheating to get by. I had no idea what normal functioning on a daily basis was all about.

"I hit rock bottom when three dope dealers beat me at gunpoint for something I didn't even do. That was when I called on Jesus and He brought me to the ARC.

"While living at The Salvation Army, I accepted

Christ as my Savior. It was August 18, 1989. I'll never forget it.

"After accepting Christ, my recovery became easier. There are still mountains to climb, but as long as I keep my faith, I'll never fear. The stability in my life began the day I found Christ.

"I thank God for leading me to the ARC, because that's where I found joy and peace. My recovery is very important and filled with fun.

"Since leaving the ARC, I have successfully experienced life, even through the hard times. My life is filled with love, joy, peace, and sharing.

"I made a vow to the Lord that I would tell of His goodness all over the world. This testimony is part of that vow."

MEDITATION: *Our God loves and is faithful. Therefore, we keep God's commandments* (Deut. 7:8-11).

PRAYER: *My stability starts with You and is completed in You, Lord. Without Your strength, I can't make it. I believe You are giving me that strength day by day.*

TWO

BEGINNING AT THE BOTTOM

Some of us seem to start life with three strikes against us. The question for us is not, "Why drink or drug?" Our question is, "Why not drink or drug?"

Even when we start sobriety, we have many wounds which still need to be healed, many sins which still need to be forgiven, many relationships which still need to be restored—and some that may never be restored. But with Jesus Christ, miracles do happen. The next stories show us that a tragic beginning doesn't always have to have an unhappy ending.

DOING DRUGS
WITH MOM

*D*onna grew up in a dysfunctional family. She says, "Although I did very well in school, my home was not a home. As I got to be a young adult, I got into drinking and drugs. I quit school and got married when I was seventeen. Drugs were my way of life, and I had two children by the age of twenty."

Donna tried to juggle keeping a job, caring for her children, and maintaining her drug addiction, but couldn't. She lost numerous jobs, was cited for child neglect, and became generally unable to deal with her life.

> As I got to be a young adult, I got into drinking and drugs.

She says that her addiction did not bring her as far down as some other people, but, "It was enough to bring me here. My mother and I smoked $600.00 a day and lost our apartment."

Since coming into recovery, Donna says, "I have really grown close to the Lord, and with Him my recovery seems to be coming along fine. Although I have only begun my recovery, with prayer and Him by my side, I feel content where I am today. I have surrendered my addiction to God, and being in the ARC reminds me of this daily."

Although Donna is very early in her process of recovery, she says, "I have pieces of myself where I thought I was lost. I am also successful at being one of the Lord's children. That in itself is a success, because once I could not remember who He was."

MEDITATION: *When we obey God, He accepts us as family. Then He is the source of our possessions, our children, and our successes in business* (Deut. 28:9-13).

PRAYER: *Lord, in Your mercy, change my misfortunes into gladness. In Your strength, show me how to be a benefit to other people again.*

BOY ARSONIST

*B*laming the victim is common in our society. When Peter was born out of wedlock to a young girl from a prominent family in a small town, her family found it hard to deal with. He was sent to an orphanage.

At the age of three, he began his tours of foster homes. He says, "I never found love in any of these homes, and I began to develop resentment toward everyone."

Peter began setting fires when he was six or seven years old. Three times he was sent to reform school to punish him for his behavior, but no one took the time to see what his real problems were.

When he was twelve, his mother found out where he was. She came with her new husband and took him to Ohio.

The man she had married drank a lot and was abusive. Peter tried to appeal to his mother, but she had mental problems of her own.

At thirteen, he began drinking. He says, "It relieved the pain and removed a lot of the guilt; I felt I was the cause of most of the problems I had in my life."

At sixteen, under the influence of alcohol, Peter attempted to kill his stepfather! He was sent to a mental hospital for the criminally insane. He stayed there until he was twenty-one years old. Regarding his time in the hospital, Peter says, "I learned to become filled with distrust and hate. Although I was a Catholic, I turned against God to the point where I probably would have put Christ on the cross myself. I began to blame God for all my problems. How could a loving God allow all these things to happen to me?"

It was while Peter was at the hospital that he first met The Salvation Army. A young lieutenant visited him and told him for the first time that God loved him.

I never found love in any of these homes.

Peter wouldn't have even been at the chapel service to hear about God's love, except that he had accepted a bribe of a carton of cigarettes to attend for someone else.

Later, after the lieutenant moved to another town, a Salvation Army captain came to visit Peter. He arranged for Peter to be sent to The Salvation Army ARC in Toledo, Ohio. This experience was not easy for either Peter or the ARC administrators. He continued to drink and cause problems for some time.

Finally, Peter says, "I figured I had more to gain than to lose by turning my life over to Christ."

That was twenty-five years ago. Peter says, "I've learned that if you make a sincere commitment to God, He will be there for you."

After an extended period of involvement with

the ARC as a resident, Peter was eventually made an employee. He later moved to the East Coast where he was employed as an ARC counselor. Since then, Peter has married and is respected in his Corps and community. He currently works for a fish-processing company in Portland, Maine.

"In all of my problems," Peter says, "I discovered that Christ was the answer. When nothing else worked, His love for me did."

MEDITATION: *Our strength, courage, and obedience to God create prosperity for us. When we meditate on Scripture, prosperity and success are the result. Our courage comes from knowing God's Presence is with us* (Josh. 1:7-9).

PRAYER: *When I am afraid, Lord, I will trust You. I believe that You can make me strong when I am weak, and rich though I am poor.*

FOURTEEN YEARS
OF HARD TIME

*O*ne of the tragedies of broken families is that children often believe they are the source of the problem. Ronald grew up with a single-parent, grandmother family but says, "It was very normal until about the fifth grade." Ron goes on to blame himself: "I became very rebellious and incorrigible. As a result, I was sent away to a boys' school and later to a reformatory."

As an adult, Ronald began to have problems with drugs: heroin, reefers, and pills. In his mid-twenties he was involved in an armed robbery that caused the death of one man and the wounding of another. He was sentenced to life in prison. After almost fifteen years, he was allowed out due to his good behavior in the institutional environment.

Ron's parole officer, a personal friend, suggested that he go to The Salvation Army ARC. He says, "Within two months I received Jesus Christ as my Savior."

Even though he had no male role model at home and the role models in prison were negative, Ron now says, "I am trying to live up to my potential as a Christian man. I am learning how to live as a person in recovery and how to be responsible for me today."

Ronald has been successful in graduating from the ARC program, and has been hired as a Salvation Army employee. He says, "It certainly is a blessing. With the help of staff and my new convictions pertaining to God, I am beginning to enjoy and love this new life that escaped me for so many years. Life began when I submitted my will and began to live by His will."

I was sent away to a boys' school and later to a reformatory.

MEDITATION: *Our purity opens the way for God's miracles* (Josh. 3:5). *God has perfect timing* (Josh. 5:12). *God responds to our faith with His mercy* (Josh. 6:25).

PRAYER: *I am willing to have You change my life, Lord. Purify me from evil desires and deeds so that I may see Your miracles at work in my life.*

MY GODS
WERE DEMONS

*J*oe never learned to read and write. He was painfully shy and filled with fear.

As a child, he had few friends. He was always afraid that other kids would hurt him.

In 1966, he got a job as a dishwasher at Duquesne University in Pittsburgh. After that, he worked as a silversmith until 1973, when the owner's business failed.

He returned to Duquesne University, where he worked in housekeeping for the next eight years, until the last of his family died.

After that, Joe lived alone. He says, "That's when I started drinking."

When his best friend, the silversmith, died also, Joe drank uncontrollably. He recalls, "I got thrown out of my house as a result of the alcohol. I didn't care about anything. My life was completely messed up.

"For a while, I just lived on the streets of Pittsburgh. I drank constantly—I was alone in the world.

"One day, I asked the newspaper boy for help. He brought me to The Salvation Army.

"By the time I arrived at the ARC, anxiety and depression had stolen my every dream. Sickness had secured my soul! I cowered at the thought of death. My gods were demons. I'd rejected everyone who had tried to help me, but secretly I hoped that someone would hear my plea for help.

"I didn't know how to pray; I never learned. God knew my heart, and it was at the ARC that I finally turned my life over to Jesus Christ.

"This was my first prayer: 'Lord, please free me from my evil ways. Drinking has led nowhere. I've lost my job, my home, my family, and my friends. Lord, I know you led me to this place. Now I won't have to be alone.'"

I asked the newspaper boy for help.

Today Joe says, "I thank God that I finally lost my fear. I am free from the spell the drinking had on me. At the ARC, I found the help and the hope that I'd only dreamed about before. I am grateful for this brand-new life that God's grace has granted me."

MEDITATION: *Like Gideon, we often question God about things that have gone wrong in our lives. Sometimes, God tells us that we are the answer, to solve the very question we have asked* (Judg. 6:11-16)!

PRAYER: *I do not understand evil in the world or tragedy in my own life, Lord. Still, I am willing to be part of the solution.*

GROWING UP
IN THE GUTTER

*D*avid was introduced to drugs and alcohol when he was twelve. He had his first overdose at thirteen, and he was sent to his first institution at fourteen.

Home life was torment. David had an abusive stepfather who made his daily life miserable. He ran away from home many times. Growing up in the streets made him accustomed to poverty and crime.

The streets became his counsel and companion. He says, "Drugs had stolen my life from me, eventually leading me to ten rehabs, state hospitals, and jail. My addiction caused me to lose my education, my job, and my family.

"My living skills were reduced to almost animal-like behavior. I hurt everyone who came into contact with me."

It was as though David was tearing himself apart from the inside. He says, "I was killing myself, but I was also trying to live.

"After I'd lost all hope in myself, I lost faith in doctors and psychiatrists. It was then that I turned to God for help.

"The Lord led me to The Salvation Army. Once

I'd accepted Jesus Christ as my Savior, my recovery began. My newfound spiritual life was hard to put into words. Worries and burdens were lifted and I felt an inner peace. I knew I was no longer alone.

"During my eleven months at the ARC in Wilkes-Barre, Pennsylvania, I learned to be patient and to keep an open mind. It was the beginning of a new life. After leaving the ARC, I continued to work for The Salvation Army. I stayed involved with the men who were still living at the Center."

My living skills were reduced to almost animal-like behavior.

David has a recipe for continuing his recovery outside of the Adult Rehabilitation Center: "I've stayed clean and sober by attending church services, going to counseling, and trusting in the Lord each day. Now I have a relationship with family, friends, and God. I am a responsible, productive member of society."

MEDITATION: *We have the right to choose to follow God* (Ruth 1:16). *Then, we act on our faith* (Ruth 1:19). *We obey spiritual authority* (Ruth 3:4). *And we reap God's reward* (Ruth 4:10).

PRAYER: *Just for today, I choose to follow You, Lord. I will do what I believe is right, and I will trust You for the outcome.*

DAD TIED ME TO A RADIATOR

*R*afael grew up in a family rampant with violence, perversion, and addiction. His father and both of his uncles were alcoholics, to whom his mother could not stand up.

Rafael was sexually abused before he was even ten by one of his cousins and was sexually abused again at age ten by one of his uncles, while his father was in the next room drinking and getting drunk, too busy to know or understand what was being done to his own son. In both instances, Rafael was told never to say anything to anyone.

Rafael's earliest recollections of his father are only of violence: "He believed in ruling with a heavy hand. He'd come home drunk and beat on us, sometimes just to rid himself of his own anger. He busted my head four times, stabbed my mother, and told me when I went back to school not to say anything or he would beat me again." So Rafael was brought up with the thought that he was never to say what was really happening in his life.

"Through all the years of abuse," Rafael says, "I was always too scared to say what had happened, or I'd make up a lie—I got very good at doing that."

Out of discipline, rage, or insanity, there were times when Rafael's father would have the children strip down to their shorts. Then he would tie them to the radiator, pour rice on the floor and make them kneel for days without any other food.

Rafael says, "I grew up with a lot of hatred and resentment, wondering, *What did I do to be treated this way?*"

Although Rafael was good in athletics at school—including football, baseball, track, and basketball—his pain and resentment made him unable to concentrate on academic studies.

I was always too scared to say what had happened.

Then, the relatively safe world of school was destroyed when, as Rafael reports, "I was sexually abused by a high school coach, which made me turn away from everything. I couldn't respect or trust anyone, and I was fully blown into my addiction, drinking on a daily basis, smoking, and skipping school. Other parents would tell their children to stay away from me because I was no good. I was a drunk, no good, a stealer, a thief, and couldn't be trusted."

Rafael was forced to move out of his house at age fifteen and actually did better on his own. He finished school with a B+ average, although he was still drinking and doing drugs because he did not like himself.

Rafael has destroyed many jobs and many relationships because of his addiction, and he holds himself responsible for his wife's death, "because I was not there when she needed me."

When his wife died, he went to the streets. "I left everything by choice because I wanted to die, but I didn't know how; but my Higher Power came to my rescue, the One who I turned my back on for so long; He never let me go. He was always there. I just didn't realize it or want to see it."

Rafael continues, "Here I was for so long giving my soul to the devil, and all the time my Higher Power was there and wouldn't let me go out that way. I am reborn; I am no longer a prisoner of myself or my addictions. For so long I didn't know who I was, where I was, or where I was going. Today I know who I am, where I am, and what I am, and how to give of myself and care for others."

MEDITATION: *We worship God regularly* (1 Sam. 1:3). *When we are upset, we pray to our God* (1 Sam. 1:10-11). *We keep on believing that God is already answering our prayers* (1 Sam. 1:19-20).

PRAYER: *Lord, I lift all my sorrow and rage up to You and ask You to melt them down to nothing in the heat of Your great love for me. Let me just put my head on Your shoulder . . . and call you . . . Father.*

DRUNK FATHER, DRUNK SON

*T*homas, like most boys, wanted to grow up to be like his dad. He succeeded by failing.

He says, "I came from a good, well-educated family. Things went well for us until my father's drinking became real bad.

"Then my mother passed away, and things went from awful to worse.

"I started hanging with the wrong group. My drinking became constant and I got into trouble with the law. I was sent to jail.

"My life was totally unmanageable. It went quickly downhill. Most of my family didn't want anything to do with me because of my drinking problems and my difficulty with the law.

"I started living with my alcoholic father. My boyhood dreams had come true—I was just like my dad. It was a nightmare!

I didn't know how to say no to a drink that was offered to me.

"I didn't know how to say no to a drink that was offered to me. Before coming to the ARC, I didn't believe in Jesus the way I believe in Him now.

"Things in my life today are better than I ever thought they could be. I don't drink anymore, and I am back in contact with my family. We see things a lot better than we ever did before—it's great!

"Since leaving the program, things are going very well for me. I attend AA meetings, and I enjoy my life without alcohol in it.

"I am grateful to The Salvation Army. The program works—if you work it."

MEDITATION: *We are learning to discern and answer the call of God* (1 Sam. 3: 2-18).

PRAYER: *I have searched for You in a bottle and needle, Lord, but I couldn't find You there. Then You came searching for me here, and You found me. Thank you.*

MOLESTED BY
MY UNCLE

When Doug was eighteen, he moved out of his house and ended up in jail, due to his drinking and drugging. His life as a young child was "great" until his mother and father separated. Then, his mother was trying to raise five children and resorted to a lot of verbal abuse in order to maintain discipline. With his mother not able to supervise the children adequately, Doug was molested by his uncle at age nine. For years after, he says, "I always felt it was my fault." So, by the time he was old enough to drive he was already drinking and getting into trouble with the law. No wonder that at age eighteen, he found himself in jail.

Later, as an adult, he lost his best friend due to drugs. Then his brother, who was a minister, and probably his closest friend, died. Doug says, "I just got to the point where I was losing my mind."

When there is great tragedy and woundedness in your life, recovery does not always come easy. Doug says, "My first ARC was in 1988 in Paterson, New Jersey. When I got there, I did not believe in God; I didn't believe in myself; but they really loved me when I couldn't love myself."

The program worked for Doug, and he stayed clean for two and a half years. Then, as he puts it, "I thought I could do it my way again."

I always felt it was my fault.

At the time he shared his story, Doug had checked himself into the Wilmington, Delaware, ARC and had begun to recreate his recovery. With only sixty days clean time, Doug still feels that he has learned about the love of God, and how it impacts his recovery: "One thing that I feel for me is that I know I no longer have to be without God in my life, and that is only due to this program. I would just like to thank God for giving me another chance and the ARC for accepting me one more time." Every sober day is a miracle!

MEDITATION: *Our God wants to be a Father to us, and to have us be His sons and daughters* (2 Sam. 7:14; 2 Cor. 6:18). *God will discipline us, but His mercy will never leave us* (2 Sam. 7:15).

PRAYER: *I am learning to tell You when I hurt, Lord. I am learning to be honest with myself as well. Give me the courage to face the pain and to lift it up and place it in Your nail-pierced hands.*

A YOUNG OLD MAN

Young adulthood never had a chance to reach me," says Warren, "I bypassed that stage and became an old man." Raised in a home with an alcoholic mother and no father, Warren was abused verbally, physically, and mentally, although he says he was never abused sexually. Often, Warren and his mother had very little to eat. Watching his mother's struggles to survive, he felt like a burden and tried to become an adult while he was still a child.

Warren began to associate with people three to four times his own age. He tried to talk like them and to become one of them. He says, "I learned how to live a life of eating, drinking, and making merry." He goes on, "It destroyed me—destroyed everything I touched—my marriage, my friendships, it even destroyed my dreams."

The most heartbreaking battle Warren lost with alcohol was when he chose to surrender to it. "Over God's call in my life to preach the Gospel. I ran and ran, until I could run no more."

Since coming to the ARC, Warren has rededicated his life to God and to the work he originally felt called by God to do. "Today," he says, "I feel stable in my walk with the Lord. I feel like, today, I won't fail. I believe that, today, I will not drink or think about drinking.

"And by the grace of God, it started right here. There is no doubt that my life's missing link appeared right here. My appointment from God to be His servant, to minister for Him, to preach and praise, is so clear today."

I ran and ran, until I could run no more.

Warren has become a Soldier of The Salvation Army, and he is praying to be used by God as a minister of the Gospel. In addition, Warren has been reunited with his wife and children and has regained his health, respect, and dignity.

According to Warren, "My success is that I have another chance; that's success for me. I enjoy life. I live today. I am so, so happy. This is real."

MEDITATION: *When we follow God, we prosper (1 Kings 2:3). Therefore, we pray for wisdom, and we receive both wisdom and prosperity. Even our health is improved as we obey God (1 Kings 3:5-15).*

PRAYER: *Lord, I am sick and tired of being sick and tired. I want to stop running and start following. I want to stop acting stupid and start being spiritually smart. Please change me.*

SUDDEN DEATH

*G*erald grew up in Detroit and never knew his father. In spite of this, he experienced love from his extended family, since his grandmother raised him (he called her "mother"), while his real mother worked to support them. An aunt and uncle were also very involved and "gave me everything I wanted until I became spoiled."

Gerald says, "I could see the love of the Lord in my family."

Then in 1986, Gerald's brother, in his mother's house, took his stepfather's rifle and shot himself in the head. Shortly thereafter, the grandmother who had raised Gerald died. Gerald was divorced from his wife of ten years and separated from the

I started to drink and drug heavy that year.

son and daughter he still loves. He explains, "I started to drink and drug heavy that year, hit bottom, but I still remembered God.

"After years of hurting myself and hitting bottom, I cried out to the Lord on April 29, 1993 in my darkest hour, and He heard me. After talking to a person about hope, I learned about the Detroit ARC and entered the program. Since I have been here, I have rejoined my relationship with Jesus and have been restored to sanity."

Gerald successfully completed The Salvation Army ARC Program and, after graduation, was hired as a production assistant. He says, "I am learning that I can live without drinking and drugging. I am making my AA/NA meetings four times a week, which is a joy. I thank the Lord that there is hope. I know who I am again."

MEDITATION: *Elijah kept on praying until it rained; we keep on praying, and our God answers* (1 Kings 18:37-45)!

PRAYER: *I remember Your love, even in my darkest hours. You, Lord, are the source of my sanity and my hope.*

THREE

THE LOW ROAD OF ADDICTION

When a chemical becomes our higher power, we are on a downhill slide to destruction. Sometimes the slide is gradual, but it always leads down. Sometimes the slide is rapid, and the pain, sin, and self-debasement come quickly and tragically.

Alcohol and other drugs are compelling, but we have found them to be evil and uncaring masters. They have led us to poverty, ruined our families, provoked us to violence, sabotaged our emotions, and destroyed our lives.

Kim's story, and those that follow, are not pretty, but they are true examples of what addiction does to us.

GOOD GIRL
GONE BAD

*K*im was raised in a middle-class family, but by age seventeen she was experimenting with alcohol and drugs, looking for a feeling to fill a void in her life. How does a "good girl" from a "good family" end up losing everything and entering the vicious world of addiction?

Kim tells us, "Anyone looking in would have thought we were your stereotypical perfect family, but we were not; we were all carrying a lot of emotional pain deep inside. When I was nine, my mother took her own life behind alcohol and an addiction to prescription drugs. My father then took on both parental roles. Although I can never remember us ever going without anything we needed, material or otherwise, I always felt alone. I had an empty feeling inside that said who I was simply was not enough. Because of my upbringing, I became the classic overachiever and people pleaser. Once I started using drugs, the not-being-enough feeling simply disappeared."

Before Kim came to Rosecrest, the ARC women's program in Fresno, California, her addiction had progressed very rapidly. She had lost everything and was caught in a vicious slide which she describes as "seeking worldly desires and using drugs, heading down a road of total destruction, with no love for myself and no self-esteem." Kim was completely alone.

Everyone has a different kind of "bottom" that signals when life is now desperate enough that recovery is better than addiction. Kim's lifestyle was so bad that her brothers were ashamed of her and decided not to invite her to a barbecue for their father on Father's Day. She says, "Because I come from a very close family, this truly crushed me."

The following Sunday, she started attending church again and that week rededicated her life to the Lord. She says, "Growing up, I attended Sunday school and church, but I had never had a real relationship with the Lord. On July 1, 1992, Kim began her program at Rosecrest. She says, "I was frightened of the unknown, but this was my first ray of hope. Quickly I got settled and began the long process of recovery and building my relationship with the Lord. Through work therapy, chapel, and various types of meetings and classes, I was able to learn tools needed for my new life of recovery. Through my six-month program, I was also able to take care of many burdens that had haunted me for years, both legal and otherwise."

Following her graduation on December 31, 1992, Kim continued to work her program and for three months was a Senior Beneficiary while obtaining more tools for transition, and at the same time looking for employment. She says that this was probably one of the most difficult steps of her recovery, "waiting for things to happen in God's time, not my own." Later she was able to be employed by The Salvation Army Family Services Agency and obtained her own car.

These were major steps toward an independent life. Kim has since moved into her own apartment and continues her family services work, about which she says, "Working in the Family Services Agency has truly been a blessing, having the opportunity to work with people from all walks of life." She particularly likes working with the women at the Chowchilla Prison, where she works with the prerelease class.

I always felt alone, with an empty feeling inside.

Today, Kim is a Soldier in The Salvation Army. Her favorite Scripture is, "Therefore, if anyone is in Christ, he is a new creation; the old has gone, the new has come" (2 Cor. 5:17 NIV). She says, "Today, life is the best it has ever been. Because of the power of Jesus Christ, and many of His faithful servants, He saved me from death and despair and gave me a new life."

MEDITATION: *We are learning to ask for help when we need it and believe God will meet us in our need* (2 Kings 4:1-7).

PRAYER: *I come to You with my aches and hurts and unhealed heart. I surrender my addictions to alcohol, sex, and drugs, which have not filled the empty spaces in my soul. Fill up the holes in my heart with Your great love.*

PLAY NOW,
PAY LATER

Jerry's ninety days were up and he was the same person he was when he entered the Center. He still had a bad temper, an arrogant attitude, and didn't care about anyone—not even himself. He knew something was wrong and that he would relapse if he left the program. He asked his counselor for another ninety days. This time, he made a commitment to himself to get involved in the program.

Jerry's mother and father were alcoholics. He was a quiet kid with eight brothers and five sisters, ashamed of his clothing and ashamed of his family.

His only outlet as a child was sports. He says, "If it wasn't for sports activities, I don't know where I would have been." The sports helped him to stay away from the house. At home, there were always parties with alcohol as the main entertainment.

Following his family's pattern, after high school Jerry began drinking and doing drugs, going to parties, and hanging out on the street corners. Because of alcohol and drugs, he dropped out of college after just three months.

Jerry describes the effects of his addiction: "My drinking and drugging caused me to lose high-income jobs, my home, family, friends. I, of course, lost myself. I was sleeping in abandoned buildings, cars, park benches, airports, or just walking the streets for entire days, not knowing where I would get my next meal, wash, or bed.

"I experienced numerous blackouts, not knowing what I did the night before. I hurt so many friends and family through my drinking and drugging, but I still didn't think I had a problem. I mentally abused my son. He couldn't think, sleep or eat without worrying about me. Finally I started to feel the pain."

My drinking and drugging caused me to lose high-income jobs, my home, family, friends.

That was when Jerry came to The Salvation Army. He came because he felt he had burned all his bridges and didn't have a place to stay. Although he almost flunked out of his first ninety days, his commitment during the second ninety days was radically different. He says, "I joined AA groups; I was Chairman, Secretary, and Treasurer. I began to seek the Lord Jesus Christ, which I found very hard. When I was out there running I'd ask the Lord for my alcohol and drugs or to get me out of this problem. I knew I could ask the Lord Jesus Christ to give me strength and guide my decisions one day at a time. Today, I find it easy to talk to God. I just thank Him morning, noon, and night."

Jerry is accepting leadership responsibility as the resident manager at the Center. His success comes through helping other men, those who have decided that they want help.

Jerry says, "I get a chance to show and tell them how it works for me. Rarely have you seen a person fail that followed our path. Today, everything is marvelous."

MEDITATION: *Our God meets our need. But Satan counterattacks when we least expect it. So we go back to God again and hold on in faith. God answers our earnest prayer. And we are grateful* (2 Kings 4:14-37).

PRAYER: *Let me never be afraid to come back to You again, Lord. You are never tired of answering my prayers.*

MY DAD
TAUGHT ME TO DRINK

*P*eter had a good Christian name, and he came from a strong hardworking family. One of the few flaws was that his father, who worked on the docks, liked to take a drink now and then.

I didn't find my way back to spiritual things until I turned from drinking.

Peter, started drinking at thirteen because he thought it was the thing to do. Once he started he didn't stop for nearly thirty years! It was then that he had to admit he was an alcoholic.

He had worked hard, like his father before him. He held one job for nine years and another for fifteen, but his drinking caught up with him. He says, "I was a member of the South Reformed Dutch Church until I was seventeen years old; but I stopped going, and I didn't find my way back to spiritual things until I turned from drinking and went to Graymoor.

Peter came from Graymoor to The Salvation Army ARC and now says, "I have been a recovering alcoholic for seven years and now attend religious services regularly."

58

Returning to his spiritual roots has been uplifting for Peter. He describes his family as having been loving and supportive during his childhood. It was simply his father's desire to have a drink that sent him the wrong signal and cost him dearly for most of his life.

Today, Peter is glad that God is a God of second chances.

MEDITATION: *Each of us needs a place of prayer* (1 Chron. 13:3). *When we do what God tells us, we succeed and are honored for it* (1 Chron. 14:14-17).

PRAYER: *Now I am finding my way back to You, through prayer and Bible study. Help me to have a regular place and time to meet with you.*

VIOLENT CHILDHOOD, VIOLENT MARRIAGE

*M*y life as a child was like that of any other child who was raised in an alcoholic home. There was constant turmoil and strife. The thing that used to upset me most was seeing my mother and stepfather carrying whiskey bottles in a sack, getting drunk and then fighting. My stepfather would urinate on himself, and my older sister would whip him like a little child.

Ernie shares with us, "On my thirteenth birthday, I tried to drink to get away from my problems. By sixteen, I was an alcoholic.

Ernie got married five years later to his childhood sweetheart, moved to Detroit, and worked at hard labor. He says, "I worked for every small moving company in Detroit." He also admits, "During our brief marriage, I got drunk and beat my wife every payday. She didn't do anything wrong; I thought you couldn't be a man unless you could give your wife a good whipping before she whipped you."

After his wife left, Ernie had a lady friend by whom he had two daughters. He says, "She finally got tired of me abusing her and the kids, so she left."

Then, in 1984, Ernie's mother died, and he added weed, crack, and cocaine to his existing addiction.

"I had forgotten about everyone else until that fateful night, May 2, 1993. I was just so tired. I got on my knees and prayed, 'Lord Jesus please help me.' I was in my girlfriend's mother's basement. I had nowhere to go, so she let me sleep in her basement. I said, 'Jesus, take me somewhere and teach me how to live.' The next morning I got up, and my girlfriend's daughter gave me two bus tickets. I used them to get myself to The Salvation Army."

I got drunk and beat my wife every payday.

Fortunately, a bad start does not have to have a bad finish. Ernie has now gained a new driver's license, has completed his GED, and has grown spiritually. He says, "This place has been wonderful for me. God has placed many good people in my life. Thank you, Jesus."

MEDITATION: *Because we are thankful, we tell everyone what God has done for us* (1 Chron. 16:7-12). *We praise our God with joy.*

PRAYER: *Thank you, Jesus, for all You have done for me. I owe You my life, and I praise You with sincere gratitude.*

ALCOHOL WAS MY MISTRESS

*G*ene's story would be pretty normal and ordinary if he hadn't discovered alcohol at age thirteen. After that, the drama became ugly, as Gene spent the next thirteen years in various jails and prisons, all due to activities tied to his alcohol addiction.

However, Gene's biggest problem was not the things that he did wrong, nor the crimes he committed and was apprehended for. As he puts it, "My biggest problem was making a commitment to anything, for any length of time, simply because alcohol ruled my life. I've been married and divorced twice, to two wonderful ladies, but alcohol was my mistress."

My biggest problem was making a commitment to anything.

At the time he shared his story with us, Gene had been sober almost two years. He has found the strength to show up and do a day's work five days a week. He has regained his self-respect.

Gene says, "Best of all, I've got a wonderful relationship with my family. I'm slowly regaining

62

their trust and renewing my faith and belief in God. For that, I'll always be indebted.

Gene is not the kind of person, even today, who puts himself forward or is showy in his testimony. He adds, "Even though I may not show it a lot, I truly love and believe in my God. My success has been in rediscovering my God and the great things he can do. All you have to do is believe."

MEDITATION: *Satan's suggestions, even when they seem tame, always have tragic consequences* (1 Chron. 21:1-28). *So, when we realize our sin, we repent. And we are grateful when God answers our prayers.*

PRAYER: *You are renewing my faith and belief, one step at a time. I am rediscovering You, and I do believe.*

RUNAWAY

*T*he best way to handle a problem is to run away from it," says James. "That's the way I dealt with my problems for years. As a result, my situation kept getting worse. I wasn't facing life; I was trying to avoid it.

"My father was a Baptist minister, and my mother was a home missionary in South Carolina. My parents taught me and my seven siblings about the importance of spiritual things in our lives.

"What they didn't explain was how badly life would turn out if we didn't follow the teachings of Jesus. When things didn't go my way, I turned from the teachings of Christ.

"After college, when I didn't get the job I wanted right away and the woman I had chosen to marry said no, I hit the bottle. Drinking and drugs kept me from working through my problems. I ran my way across the U.S.—in and out of countless failed relationships.

"Finally I moved to Paterson, New Jersey. It was there that I met The Salvation Army. For eleven years after that, I tried to work the program I had been taught, but I still struggled with my self will. I was near the things of God, but far away from surrendering to Him.

"It wasn't until I entered the Army's program in Jersey City that I decided to stop running. When I faced my problems and my addiction by asking God for His help, things changed. When I got back into God's program for my life, my confusion ended.

"Today, I have Jesus Christ in my life. He has given me peace in my heart. I've come home to South Carolina to my own home. My family respects me, and I have true friends again. Running away and doing life alone didn't work; following Christ and His teachings does."

When I didn't get the job I wanted right away and the woman I had chosen to marry said no, I hit the bottle.

MEDITATION: *When we forsake God, we open ourselves to defeat but when we humble ourselves and seek God, we find deliverance* (2 Chron. 12:5-12), *and things begin to work out right.*

PRAYER: *Near is not good enough for me, Lord. I want to be fully surrendered to You. As I respect Your laws, other people will respect me.*

THE NIGHTMARE
EVERY PARENT FEARS

*C*harlie was the nightmare that every parent fears. He was the drunk driver who killed a five-year-old child in a car crash!

By age 18 I was a full-blown alcoholic.

What caused a young man, born and raised in Brooklyn with a good childhood and caring parents, to become a drunk driver? Charlie's father was an alcoholic. Charlie's father introduced Charlie to alcohol at age sixteen. "By the time I could vote," Charlie says, "I was a full-blown alcoholic."

You might think that the car crash and causing the death of a child would have scared Charlie into sobriety, but it had just the opposite effect. He drank even more to take away his grief, sorrow, and guilt.

Now at the ARC, Charlie is beginning work on spiritual principles for a sane and stable life. He says, "Here, I was introduced to God and turned my life over to Him. I am building a personal relationship with God through church attendance and reading the Bible."

Is Charlie ready to be out on his own, to live a

stable, sober existence? Not yet. Charlie is honest enough about being in the early stages of his recovery to say, "I'm still in the ARC and will continue to stay here until I'm totally in touch with God."

MEDITATION: *When we do not rely on God, we lose; when we rely on God, we win. If we rely on God consistently, we will have all we need* (2 Chron. 16:7-9; 17:3-5).

PRAYER: *I'm trying to be honest with You and with myself and with other people, Lord. It isn't very easy, and I'm not doing as well as I'd like. Please help me.*

LIVED TO
GET HIGH

*D*an is now twenty-five. He started doing drugs more than half his lifetime ago.

He says, "I've used drugs by needle, pills, snorting, and smoking—any way I could get them.

He failed his way through drug programs in the early '90s. "The last go-round," he says, "was too painful. I had to stop feeding this addiction. My dignity was lost. I was humbled and guilt had set in. I was out of control. I could no longer function on my own.

I was out of control. I could no longer function on my own.

"I'd come from a very functional family. I was the middle child and only boy in a family of four. I'm a Baptist. I belong to the Elizabeth Baptist Church in Youngstown, Ohio. I graduated from Wilson High School in 1986. From there I took up a trade as a welder. I've been a worker for most of my young life. I received my forklift license in 1991." But drugs were obviously eroding Dan's normal functioning.

When he lost control in 1992, he entered the ARC in Youngstown. He says, "I was given a chance to start life over. At the ARC, I gained back the essentials that are needed to deal with life on life's terms. I found spirituality. I now have a structure to build a successful life upon.

"I thank God that I found peace. It's what I needed to accomplish my goals."

MEDITATION: *We pray to God morning and evening* (Ezra 3:2-3), *and, when we start a new job, we dedicate it to God with music and singing* (Ezra 3:10-11).

PRAYER: *I am just learning how to pray, Lord. Please filter out my mistakes and hear the deep desires of my heart. Your peace is my heart's deepest desire.*

B. A. IN
BOOZOLOGY

Although Jim is a 1977 college graduate from Tulsa University, the alcohol addiction which he started in high school as a peer-group thing caught up with him and robbed him of the success promised by his college degree.

Growing up, alcohol was always available around his home. Jim's use of alcohol led to addiction, and his addiction provided him with a "walk away instead of face the music" attitude, which undermined many important areas of his life.

I walked away with a bottle in my hands.

By 1981, Jim was divorced and had lost contact with his wife and two daughters. He says, "I walked away with a bottle in my hands."

After that, he bounced around the country for eleven years, although he did spend a fair amount of time in Reno, Nevada.

The tragedy is that Jim was brought up in the Methodist Church. He says, "I turned away from the Lord, for supposed monetary and earthly gain, after high school. I finally returned to the

Lord when I got fed up with copping out and picking up and falling down. I finally decided to seek help in June, 1992.

About his recovery, Jim says, "It's an ongoing process. The harder I work at my personal recovery, the more success I have. My best days are still down the road."

MEDITATION: *Because we believe that God rewards us with prosperity, we are willing to work* (Neh. 2:20). *We are diligent in our work* (Neh. 3:20). *We work, and pray, and watch* (Neh. 4:6, 9).

PRAYER: *I'm putting my shoulder to the wheel, Lord, and I thank you for the strength to be able to go to work today.*

TRAPPED IN
A COMPACTOR!

*I*t took a lot for Gregory to come in from the cold and embark on the process of recovery. This is his experience:

"It was cold outside, and I was shaking physically from the withdrawal of the alcohol. At this point I was bankrupt in all areas. I felt really depressed and totally unloved. I felt remorse and lot of guilt and shame. I felt really dirty, and it was about 2:00 A.M. I prayed out to God. I said, 'Lord, I don't want this no more, I have no hope. Lord, if You might see just a little good in me somewhere in all of this filth, please take the good away, if there is any, and give it to someone that needs it. Please kill the rest.' The wind started picking up after that and I got a little colder. I saw a Dumpster, went over to it, and opened the door. There was nothing inside except cardboard. I got inside the Dumpster and dozed off. The next thing I heard was the garbage truck. As it hooked onto the Dumpster, I jumped up and tried the door. It would not open. The next thing I realized, it was dumping me in with the rest of the trash. I was yelling at the top of my lungs, and the driver

72

seemed to pay no attention. I would imagine he didn't hear me over the noise of the engine.

"Once inside the truck, I thought and remembered the prayer from before. Then, I realized the driver had turned on the compactor. I remember saying, 'Lord, I realize I need Your help very bad, and if you could please stop this compactor I have changed my mind; I want to live.' The walls started getting closer and closer. I was all balled up and a piece of pipe had penetrated through my arm. Then I began to yell 'Hey Lord, I know you are listening, please, please stop these walls!'

"All of a sudden the walls stopped. They started going back into their original position. At that time, I noticed the ledge right above the cab of the truck. I climbed on top of the garbage, grabbed ahold of the ledge, and pulled myself up. Then I slid down the top of the windshield and fell to the ground, hurting my legs in the process. My arm was still bleeding. The driver couldn't believe what he had just seen. He got on his radio and called for help.

"One of the paramedics knew my sister. God started working with me immediately by introducing me to what humility feels like. I overheard the driver talking to one of the policemen. I heard him say, 'The usual truck that ran that route had engine trouble that morning and it was a newer model. It has a two-ton pressure compactor that would not have stopped.' If it had come that morning, I would be dead for sure."

Gregory's family had taught him right from wrong as he was growing up. He had had respect, hopes and dreams for the future. He started going against those principles when he made the decision to start drinking. He says, "The drink took all of my insecurities away. And when under the influence, in my own mind, I was king for the day." He says, "Money and the drink became my new gods. I sold my soul and served my life to money and to the drink all the way down to the gates of hell and the price of my own sanity."

Lord, I don't want this no more, I have no hope.

The first words Gregory remembers, after coming to the ARC, were spoken by a Salvation Army major. "The Salvation Army has been working with drug addicts, alcoholics, and behavioral problems for about one hundred years. My wife and I have been doing it for thirty years now, give or take a month or so." Then the major said, "It has to do with change. Something is broken with you, or you wouldn't be in this Center." Gregory says that he was so grateful that he heard that one word, *Change*. Gregory says, "That was an offering of hope to me."

With the help of the staff, fellow residents, and employees, along with a strong commitment to the Twelve Steps, Gregory says, "I am no longer the person I was when I came through these doors."

Today Gregory has his self-respect, his self-esteem, his hope and faith back. He can say, "I have dreams and hopes for the future. My family ties are a lot healthier and the communication lines are flowing. Today I like Greg, and I thank God for who he is becoming."

MEDITATION: *When we disobey, our God is always ready to pardon and restore us. God has great patience with us, but there are consequences if we continue in sin* (Neh. 9:16-30). *So, we recommit ourselves to follow God's law completely* (Neh. 10:29).

PRAYER: *I want to live, Lord. It doesn't need to be a dramatic life, but I would like my self-respect back. All my hope and my faith is in You, Lord.*

FOUR

ATTEMPTING RECOVERY WITHOUT JESUS CHRIST

We do not say that no one can be sober without Jesus Christ. After all, there are many nondrinkers and nondruggers who are not Christians, as well as moderate drinkers who have never become addicted.

We can only share our own experiences. And our experiences have been that many men and women come to the ARCs who have been in long-term counseling, lived in therapeutic communities, or were admitted to (one or many) hospital-based treatment programs. Many of us were not able to find or maintain our sobriety, even with all the help we received. Then, at the ARC, we chose Jesus Christ, the Son of God, to be our Higher Power.

That is what Alex and others have done. Here are their stories.

PHARMACIST JUNKIE

I checked into a Pittsburgh hospital for detox," says Alex. "This led to a total of six months in the hospital and two secular rehabs. Even after these two rehabs, I didn't have the peace that I thought would come when the addiction ended. While I was at the second secular rehab, they suggested I come to the ARC. Since I had no other choice, I accepted."

Alex's story began in a small town in southwestern Pennsylvania. He was born and grew up in the same town, but began using drugs at the early age of fourteen. By the time he was eighteen, he had progressed to using $100 of heroin a day. He was placed on methadone maintenance at age nineteen. For the next eight years, he was out of control completely with drug use.

Alex had become a pharmacy student in college and was convicted of stealing drugs from the drug company where he worked as an intern. He lost numerous jobs and also lost his marriage. Before he came to detox, he was ready to take his own life.

Alex says, "I believe God began to move in my

life while I was in the hospital. I had asked God with tears in my eyes to change me, as I could not continue to live like I was." When he finished his stay in the hospital and the secular detoxes, he still did not have a "peace that the madness was over."

I had asked God with tears in my eyes to change me, as I could not continue to live like I was.

The peace came on December 31, 1987, at a special New Year's Eve Watchnight Service conducted by the ARC. Alex remembers it as "the first time in my life I had heard about Christ's redemption through the Cross. I asked Jesus into my heart that night."

At The Salvation Army, Alex was able to stabilize his newfound faith in Jesus Christ, to begin his process of recovery, and to begin his reentry into the world of work.

Today Alex is the Director of Drug and Alcohol Services for a mental-health agency in Pittsburgh. He has married a beautiful young woman with two children, and he has found a stable and spiritually uplifting church home. Now in his ninth year of sobriety, Alex says, "I have a content life through God's grace in Jesus, and I am growing in the Lord day by day."

MEDITATION: *When we experience the attack of evil* (Esther 3:9), *we respond with personal prayer and faith* (Esther 4:1).

PRAYER: *I pray that every evil compulsion and addictive force in my life shall be reversed, Lord. And I pray that You will make me an agent of change for God and for good.*

HAD A GOOD JOB,
BUT COULDN'T KEEP IT

*G*ilford and his five brothers and sisters were raised in a Christian home. Sunday meant church, but that didn't stop him, at age fourteen, from trying a joint of marijuana or, soon after, experiencing alcohol with his friends. At the "old" age of seventeen, he tried cocaine and found himself hooked on a habit that would possess him for the next twenty-five years.

Finally, I was forced to resign before I got fired.

Gil had good jobs with the New York Times, Simon and Schuster, and finally as a conductor with the New York Transit Authority for eleven years. As he became aware of his addiction, he asked for and received treatment, but the treatment was not based on Jesus Christ, and he relapsed several times. He says, "Finally, I was forced to resign before I got fired."

Gil arrived at the Albany, New York, ARC on January 30, 1992. Many hands reached out to welcome and help him, and he was able to make some of the truest friends he has ever had in his life. Gil says that it was the spiritual aspects of this program—establishing a regular prayer life, reading and studying the Bible—that brought him to the Lord, who died to set him free.

Gil, now living on his own as a productive resident of the City of Albany, says, "The problems are still there, the pressures, the bills, the temptations, but it's what you do—you have to have God in your life. You need church and friends to make it.

MEDITATION: *Even when we are regular in our prayers and are upright in our walk, Satan is still persistent in trying to destroy us. In our troubles, we may even curse the day of our birth, but God wants to restore everything that Satan has stolen out of our lives* (Job 1; 42:10-17).

PRAYER: *Lord, help me to know that every good and perfect gift comes from You, and that You are not the author of anything evil or ugly which has come into my life. I trust Your goodness to me.*

THIRD-GRADE DRUNK

I started drinking when I was eight, and it became an everyday habit by the time I was thirteen," says John. "Also drugs came into the picture at this time." John was never in trouble with the law because his father was a police officer, although both his father and mother had drinking problems.

John says, "Despite all the craziness surrounding our family, there was also a lot of unity. When there was a crisis in our family, such as the death [of his brother in the Vietnam War] or when we lost our house to a fire, my family, including all my relatives, stuck close together."

John's background was a mixed one, including both family unity and addiction. He had entered three detox centers and several rehabs by the age of twenty-two, but, he says, "I never felt a closeness with the Lord, even though I was raised a Roman Catholic and was an altar boy."

John's longest period of sobriety was three years. The very day he started drinking and drugging again, he was arrested for drugs and sentenced to one year in jail. John says, "At this point in my life, I had nothing to live for."

John entered the ARC right after he was released from jail. He says that six months after coming to the ARC, "I asked Jesus Christ to enter my life and forgive me for my sins."

John's mixture of sanity and craziness still persisted, and he relapsed twice during the next three years, but each time he came back to God and sobriety.

At this point in my life, I had nothing to live for.

At the time he shared his story with us, John was planning to be enrolled as a Salvation Army Soldier and was also planning to go to school for computer training. John says that the key came when, through God's help, "I was able to forgive myself and get on with my life."

MEDITATION: *The Lord hears us when we call on Him. We reach our highest and best when we follow God* (Ps. 3).

PRAYER: *Forgive me, and forgive me, and forgive me, Lord, until I am able to forgive myself. It is only through Your love that I can become all of what You planned for me to be.*

NO LUCK
WITHOUT JESUS

*G*ary says, "I was so tired of living and yet too scared to die. I tried rehab after rehab with no luck, until I came to the Detroit ARC."

When Gary was a child, he thought it was normal to move around frequently, moving in and out with different relatives. He says, "We did this for quite a while until one of my father's Navy buddies got my father a job as a milkman. Once he got this job, we settled down in Detroit."

Gary continues, "My father and mother had been drinking for as long as I could remember. I started drinking at a very early age, about ten. I also remember my parents fighting all the time. I got very scared listening to them yell and hit each other. To escape this, I started smoking pot. As I look back now, that was the only way I could deal with my life at home."

Gary ran away several times, and each time he came home, his parents promised him that things would get better, but they never did. Between ages twelve and sixteen, he started drinking more and experimented with different kinds of drugs to cope with his life.

"I truly believe that by the time I was sixteen years old I was a full-blown addict, both drugs and alcohol. As I got older, the problems caused by my drinking and using continued to landslide, until nobody wanted to be near me."

Gary knew he had a problem, and he was willing to seek help for that problem, but the rehabs he tried did not introduce him to Jesus Christ, until he came to the ARC.

The problems caused by my drinking and using continued to landslide.

Gary says, "The Salvation Army has shown me that I don't have to use or drink to cope with my life. They showed me there is a true God who loves me, likes me, and cares about me very much. This has changed my whole life."

MEDITATION: *Give ear to my words, O Lord, consider my meditation. Harken unto the voice of my cry, my King, and my God: for unto thee will I pray. My voice shalt thou hear in the morning, O Lord: in the morning will I direct my prayer unto thee, and will look up* (Ps. 5:1-3 KJV).

PRAYER: *O Lord, I know that You love me, like me, and care about me very much. I feel this every time I pray to You. Thank you.*

FLUNKED OUT OF
FORTY DETOXES

*O*ver a twenty-year period, Dennis existed from day to day drugging and drinking. He claims, "The alcohol, in particular, broke me down physically, emotionally, and spiritually." Dennis was in and out of hospitals, near death twice, was put in mental institutions in which he was suicidal, went to over forty detoxes and through the twenty-eight-day program at four rehabs but never was able to remain sober. His was the ultimate hopelessness of alcoholism. He was unable to maintain any relationships, he had no friends, and he was diagnosed antisocial. Without Jesus Christ, he had no hope at all.

What kind of background led to these years of living hell?

Dennis was the older of two sons of loving but alcoholic parents. His father was paralyzed when Dennis was ten years old, due directly to alcoholism. His father only lived five more years, and his mother's alcohol consumption continued to increase. Then his mother died of hepatitis at age 54. With no real authority figure present, Dennis's drinking began. He was kicked out of high school and enlisted in the U. S. Marine Corps at age seventeen, where he began heavy drug use. Sent to Vietnam in 1969, his drug use skyrocketed in that atmosphere. Dennis was given an undesirable discharge in 1970 and went to work in an Atlantic City liquor store. His twenty years of bare existence had begun.

With a background like Dennis's, no one could blame a psychologist who would consider him incurable, but God was not ready to give up on Dennis. Dennis began the process himself; he says, "I prayed that the Lord would tear down my walls of self-will and doubt, and praise Him, He did." Dennis was born again as a new Christian at a special holiness retreat held for ARC delegates at The Salvation Army's beautiful Ladore Lodge in Pennsylvania. Dennis says, "With Jesus in my heart came the ability to fully feel God's love and saving grace. Seeking to do God's will through prayer, Bible study, and fellowship has created a new confidence to meet life's challenges soberly."

Dennis has been sober now for more than two years and employed full-time for more than eighteen months. Nine months ago he was married to a beautiful woman, a Salvation Army Soldier whom he met at the local Corps. Dennis says, "We are both very active in the Corps, share a Christian marriage, and thank the Lord daily

I prayed that the Lord would tear down my walls of self-will and doubt.

for His love and the many ways He blesses our lives."

MEDITATION: *The Lord hears and receives our prayers* (Ps. 6:1-10). *He has power over our enemies* (Ps. 6:10). *God will save us and deliver us; we trust Him* (Ps. 7:1).

PRAYER: *Jesus, hear my prayer. Save me from self-will and doubt, and give me the godly confidence I need to meet the challenges of life.*

ALWAYS SOMETHING MISSING

Andy comes from a family of alcoholics, but he is able to say, "My childhood was a happy one. Mom was loving, and Dad and I spent quality time together. He was a railroad man and didn't get home much, but our time together was special. I was brought up Catholic and attended a Catholic school.

I truly believe that I was led by God to the ARC.

Andy's mother and father were both alcoholics, and his dad died at fifty-three, when Andy was ten. His mother had to sell the house and move to an apartment in the house which Andy's aunt and uncle owned. His aunt and uncle were also alcoholics; his uncle died of alcoholism in 1988, while his aunt became involved with Alcoholics Anonymous and has been sober since 1979.

Andy made a number of attempts at recovery which failed. His diagnosis of these failed attempts is that, "There was always something missing in my attempts at recovery—that was the Lord."

He continues, "I truly believe that I was led by God to the ARC. I entered the program in June of 1992. Slowly, I started praying and thanking God for the blessings in my life. I truly believe that the Holy Spirit entered my heart when I went on retreat."

Andy is evidence that recovery is possible, but he's also proof that it is not a sure thing. He says, "I had a slip while I was here, took my will back, and picked up. I thank God that He carried my soul for that time. Now, I'm working in my program more vigorously and feeling blessed and comforted by that. With God's help, I will be able to walk the path of salvation and sobriety."

MEDITATION: *God is the protector and provider in whom we can trust* (Ps. 23:1-6).

PRAYER: *Thank you, Lord, for the blessings in my life. I believe that You will continue to help me walk the path of salvation and sobriety.*

STREET-GANG MEMBER

*C*laude is the oldest of six children. His father left home when Claude was only ten. By age fourteen, he had become a street-gang member. He began drinking when he was old enough to drive.

"Through the years," Claude says, "my drinking took me away from my emotional problems. Drinking led to drugs and, finally, to crack cocaine. In June of 1989, I had been in recovery for two months, but I did not have Jesus Christ in my life and I relapsed.

"Looking back, I think of Luke 11:24-26, where Jesus talks about the unclean spirit that goes out of a man but doesn't find any rest and says, 'I will return to my house from which I came.'" Claude says, "My condition was bad and I was homeless. Then I asked Jesus for help. The Holy Spirit led me to the Brooklyn ARC."

My condition was bad and I was homeless. Then I asked Jesus for help.

At the ARC, Claude says, "I learned of God's love for me. I became a recovering soul."

Claude now has three years of sobriety under his belt and was recently married in the ARC. Although he now has a new life in the community, he frequently can be seen at the ARC, coming back to help others find the Lord Jesus Christ.

MEDITATION: *The Lord hears us and solves the problems we can't solve* (Ps. 34:6-10).

PRAYER: *Fill my heart and soul with Your overflowing love, Lord. Then there will be no room for anything evil to creep in and destroy me again.*

MARRIAGE WAS NOT THE CURE

*F*rancis's father was an iceman. Francis was an outlaw. He skipped school, broke into houses, and robbed people. He stole from stores and businesses. By age eleven he had been in court twenty-five times, and he was sent to reform school off and on until the he was sixteen.

Francis started his addiction early: "I was drinking on my father's knee from a very young age.

After he turned sixteen, Francis started running from himself, drinking and working his way all over the country.

Ten years later, Francis got married and settled down for a while but, he says, "then I let the stress get to me. I left my wife and kids and ran around again, drinking. I had blackouts and forgetfulness. It made me so afraid that I started looking for a stabilizer. I began looking for something to help me get back my sanity, my life, and my family.

> I began looking for something to help me get back my sanity, my life, and my family.

It took Francis another five years to find out that what he needed was Christ in his life. He says, "He was with me all the time, but I would not take Him in. When I did let Jesus in, everything changed. I was loved and could love again—and not be afraid.

Today, Francis has regained the sanity, stable life, and family for which he yearned. He says, "Jesus gave me new hope, a new life, self-respect, and my family back. Jesus is the greatest part of my life."

MEDITATION: *Oh wash me, cleanse me from this guilt. Let me be pure again. For I admit my shameful deed—it haunts me day and night* (Ps 51:2-3 TLB).

PRAYER: *Create a clean heart in me, O Lord. Restore the joy of Your salvation in me. Deliver me from guilt.*

FROM STREET KID
TO STREET BUM

After a dozen years of sobriety in AA, Tommy met another woman and divorced his wife. He couldn't handle the guilt and traded his sobriety for drink again. Although he had some periods of sobriety after that, he always went back to drinking. He says, "I needed more than AA to help me handle my guilt. I was a real bum."

Tommy's father had been an alcoholic who contracted TB and spent seven years in a TB hospital. While he was away, Tommy was a street kid who hung out with a gang, which was when he started drinking. He says, "My mother was a weak woman, and as the oldest of four children, I was more or less on my own. My father eventually died of his alcoholism." Tommy was already an alcoholic by the time of his first marriage.

I was on the street off and on; a real bum.

Tommy was not able to reestablish his sobriety until he worked at a closer relationship with Christ through the Army's program. He says that The Salvation Army worship has made him feel more "comfortable and closer to God."

Recently, Tommy became an Adherent member of The Salvation Army Church. He says, "I hope I can stay sober, one day at a time, with the help of God and the AA Program."

MEDITATION: *We make it a point to seek and listen to wise counsel* (Prov. 1:5); *then we trust our God to direct our journey* (Prov. 3:5-6).

PRAYER: *Please help me to walk faithfully, each step of the way, one day at a time.*

I THOUGHT
GOD WANTED ME TO BE
AN ALCOHOLIC

*J*acob says, "When I was growing up, I was reserved and shy. No one would pay much attention to me when I spoke or even pick me to be on their team when we played games. My mother and father divorced when I was about three years old and left me and my three sisters to be raised by my aunt and grandmother. My aunt and grandmother were very religious, so they involved us in lots of church activities."

He continues, "As I grew older and became a young man, I grew apart from the Lord, and from my family and friends. I got into the drug scene and made new friends, the kind that knew the streets and all the angles on how to get money to support our drug habits. It wasn't long before I became a criminal and was wanted in three states. Jacob tried to sober up, but after numerous detoxes and rehabs, countless counseling sessions, AA meetings, NA meetings, psychiatrists, and medications, he knew why he was the way he was and how he got that way. However, he says, "With my newfound wisdom and all the energy I could muster, I was powerless to change who or what I was." He says, "I even called on the Lord, time and time again. Still no relief came."

Jacob finally decided that if he could not figure it out, and if the Lord does answer prayer, the Lord must want him to be an alcoholic as a ministry for someone else, or as an example of how not to be and what not to do. Today he says, "That was pretty twisted thinking, but with that I quit trying. I gave up." Before getting out of the detox he was in, someone suggested that he go to The Salvation Army ARC in Wichita, Kansas, to recuperate from his latest dive. This one had lasted nine months, drinking a minimum of a quart of whiskey per day. He reluctantly went, thinking it would be just another flophouse.

Jacob reports, "Since day one here at The Salvation Army, things started to happen. Without my noticing it at first, the compulsion to drink and drug had been totally lifted from me. My first weekend here I was allowed to go to a weekend campout and revival which the Salvation Army sponsors annually. This privilege was usually reserved for residents with more seniority than I had. During that weekend, the chaplain and I had some serious conversations about the Lord; later he convinced me to read the Scriptures and get some answers.

"Since I started reading, I haven't been able to put the Word down—and I hate to read! Shortly after that I made a deal with the Lord. If He would help me quit smoking, I would read Scripture every time I got the urge to smoke and not quit until the urge went away. Well, in the last nine months, I have read the Bible from cover to cover twice and the New Testament at least four times besides. Yet never once have I had to read Scripture because of an urge to smoke!"

I could not change who or what I was.

Since God has entered his life, Jacob says, "My legal problems have all been resolved, except for a few fines I have to pay. The blessings go on and on."

Jacob decided that he would stay at the Center "as long as the Lord will allow, in order to help others find what I have found— Jesus."

MEDITATION: *Wisdom is the ultimate attainment of a spiritual life. God is teaching and instructing and leading us to walk and run successfully; our job is to listen, receive, and take firm hold of what He is teaching* (Prov. 4:7-13).

PRAYER: *Thank you, Lord, for all you are doing for me. Your Word is becoming more valuable to me each day. Your counsel and guidance are very valuable to me.*

FIVE

DISCOVERING THE ARC

Some of us found the ARC the hard way—right out of prison! Some of us had a "coincidence" and walked into a building we hadn't even known existed. Some heard about the ARC from friends who were successful graduates. And some heard from people in the street who had relapsed.

But we all came. And were surprised by love—the love of the officers and staff, the love of the other residents, the love of Jesus.

FROM ADDICT
TO EDITOR

At the Lytton, California, ARC, I found a reawakening of that which is in all of us. The walls of old ideas and habits were torn down, and a new, solid foundation was laid through solid teaching and guidance.

Bruce continues, "I began to feel wrongs which had never bothered me before. I was beginning to care about myself and others. The feeling of peace, through Jesus Christ, overwhelmed me. He had never left me! The wholeness I'd been looking for all these years was finally mine."

Bruce had been brought up in a Christian family but had come to take God for granted. Having only a shaky foundation to build on, his morals and values declined, and he found himself using more and more drugs and alcohol. His professional career was over, and as he puts it, "The fall downward was swift."

He was blaming everything on everyone else, not admitting his own problems with drugs. Eventually, Bruce was arrested and charged with seven drug felonies. Rather than sending him to prison, the judge had the insight to send him to the ARC for rehabilitation.

At the Lytton ARC, Bruce found Jesus Christ as the core of his recovery. His addiction and self-centeredness have been replaced by a new concern for God and others.

I was beginning to care about myself and others.

He says, "Now that I am out of the Center, my life has taken a whole new twist. My concern is for others, expressed by my involvement in drug awareness. I am even a local editor of a paper that informs the public (circulation 40,000 plus) of prevention events, activities, and concepts."

What is most important to Bruce now? "That I get to share with those who are hurting the spirituality of recovery. Thank you, Lord!"

MEDITATION: *We know that alcohol and other drugs increase bad times, sadness, quarreling, complaining, and hurt feelings* (Prov. 23:29-32).

PRAYER: *I know that my strength, power, and safety come from You, Lord. I pray that You will also increase in me the gifts of wisdom and discernment.*

THE ARC IN MY NEIGHBORHOOD

I grew up a few blocks from the ARC. During my childhood, I never even noticed the building! The last thing I ever thought was that someday I would call it home.

"In high school, I began smoking marijuana. Later, during the '70s, I moved toward other drugs. I did mescaline, THC, lonnigenol, and acid. After micodots and sniffing powdered cocaine, I graduated to freebasing cocaine.

"During my active drug use, I gave away the trust of my family and friends.

"I've been stabbed, hit with a baseball bat, and physically beaten several times. I was also locked up in jail a couple of times.

I learned what I should do, instead of chasing after what I wanted to do.

"When I finally took an honest look at myself, I wanted something more than drugs! I reached out for help. The ARC was one of the steps along the way to life again. It was a tool to move me from 'mere existence' to living. For eight months, I was a resident of the ARC in Toledo, Ohio. I learned to recognize what I should do, instead of chasing after what I wanted to do."

Today, John describes himself as a "tax-paying member of society." He is employed by one of the social agencies that helped him along the way.

As John understands his situation, "I can never repay my debt to the ARC and the other agencies that helped me. I am told that God works through people. Maybe I can be one of His instruments."

MEDITATION: *We expect to do our work before we reap the rewards* (Prov. 24:27). *When we hold each other accountable, we do it gently and precisely* (Prov. 25:12-14).

PRAYER: *Use me, O Lord, to be an instrument of Your peace. Where there is hatred, let me show love; where there is discord, let me bring harmony.*

WHEN THE
FOG LIFTED

*B*efore entering the ARC, my life was unmanageable," states Willie. "I was sharing an apartment with a friend who still uses cocaine on a daily basis. I had no job and had no desire to get one. I lived each week waiting for my state check. I did not pray or go to church."

Willie's new life began when he entered the ARC. He has always had a non-specific Christian faith. He says, "I found Jesus again when the fog lifted in my head. I asked His forgiveness of my sins. I asked God to take control of my life."

> I found Jesus again when the fog lifted in my head.

Today, Willie's recovery process is based on working the Spiritual principles of the Twelve steps into his life. He is reversing the process of drug and alcohol abuse that started at the end of eleventh grade.

Willie has become an intake clerk for the ARC. He proudly says, "I help new clients get into the ARC. I show them what this program can do for them. This program helped me to become the best person I possibly can be."

MEDITATION: *Holy living creates confidence* (Prov. 28:1-7).

PRAYER: *Continue Your control over my life, Lord. Open doors of opportunity that no man can shut, and shut tight any false doors which lead to detours away from Your will for my life.*

"USELESS"

*K*arl grew up in a dysfunctional family. His mother did everything in her power to give him and his sisters a wonderful life, but his father was an alcoholic. Because of that alcoholism, his parents were eventually divorced.

When Karl's father did come to visit the children, he would take them out drinking. The kids would have to spend their time with him in the bar, while he was constantly drunk.

By the time Karl got to junior high school, he decided that, "I wouldn't drink like my father, so I started by smoking marijuana. By the time I graduated from high school, I was drinking *and* smoking marijuana.

Karl shares, "My addiction led me to ends I thought would never be possible. My marijuana smoking led to any and all other drugs. Along with alcohol, cocaine became a big part of my addiction and caused me to steal, lie, and devastate my family.

"I became useless to myself and society. I slept on park benches and literally lived on the street. I ended up in a shelter with nothing and no hope.

And then, around the corner from the shelter, I found a Salvation Army ARC.

"Coming to the Adult Rehabilitation Center, I first felt hopeless and very scared. After a few days, hope began to settle in slowly. With the guidance of the counselors here, the Major and his wife, and their spiritual guidance, restoration began in my life.

And then, around the corner from the shelter, I found a Salvation Army ARC

"I had always known who God was, but coming to the Center allowed God to work freely without the distractions of the outside world. Here my faith and trust were strengthened."

Karl feels that his feet are now firmly placed on the recovery path and his spiritual foundation is laid.

Karl has gained his family back, and some good friends as well. He has had the opportunity to be the music director for his Center as well as a dispatcher. As Karl puts it, "In my year at the Center, God has opened doors for me that I never thought could be opened again. Restoration never would have been possible without His help, guidance, and most of all, His love and power.

MEDITATION: *We trust the criticisms of a friend more than the complements of an enemy* (Prov. 27:5-6). *Frank discussions improve our friendships* (Prov. 27:17).

"Useless"

PRAYER: *You are my greatest friend, Lord, and I am also coming to know and trust others who are following You. Help me to open myself up to godly friendships.*

BROKE A WINDOW
TO FIND JESUS

*O*ne afternoon, having sold his coat to buy crack and hurrying down the street wearing only a T-shirt and trousers, Peter heard the greeting, "Merry Christmas" and realized that it was the Christmas season, his birthday, and it was snowing—things that had totally escaped him in his love affair with crack. Peter had come a long way, the wrong way.

Peter had begun using cocaine at age eighteen. No one else knew. He married, had children, and owned his own successful business. As more and more material success came, so did increasing use of drugs. At fifty-one years of age, he tried crack cocaine and was immediately addicted.

His addiction took over more of his life. His habit cost over $200 a day for cocaine, crack cocaine, marijuana, heroin, and alcohol. Eventually his dependence caused him to choose drugs over his marriage of twenty-eight years, his home, his children, and his business. As Peter explains it, "I lost the sense of being a human being." His residence became abandoned buildings and an abandoned self.

One day he knew he had to do something.

114

After smoking his drug, he broke a store window in order to get arrested. He just wanted to be in a warm place.

From Rikers Island Prison, Peter arranged to enter a Salvation Army Rehabilitation Center and on his first Sunday responded to the message of the miracle of salvation. Peter says, "I was counseled to have hope and faith every day, and things would get better."

I lost the sense of being a human being.

Peter has now been sober and drug free for five years. He has his own apartment and a steady job. He has become a uniformed Salvation Army Soldier and says, "Jesus has changed my whole outlook on life. I know that the key to successful living is to trust Jesus. He is the power in my life."

MEDITATION: *We no longer fear men, because we trust in God. We trust our God, and He protects us* (Prov. 29:25; 30:5).

PRAYER: *I want to live successfully, Lord, as a Christian and not as a dope fiend or a drunk. Help me to live a life that shows Your beauty and love to others.*

FOUND A
BALANCED LIFE

*H*ank's "religion" was hard work. He was born into a steelworking family in Youngstown, Ohio, and was raised on the strong Protestant work ethic. Early on he learned the absolute necessity of hard work. After graduating from high school, he followed the rest of his ancestors into the steel mill.

Stability is the key that was missing in my irrational behavior.

But hard work was not enough for Hank. Addiction to alcohol and other chemicals is not the only type of problem that brings a man or woman to the ARC. Hank says, "My problems began with the onset of a chemical imbalance called manic depression. This problem sent me on a roller coaster of mood swings that eventually left me homeless, hospitalized, and imprisoned."

Hank says, "Stability is the key that was missing in my irrational behavior. This could only be achieved through a combination of medicine, meaningful work, and self-honesty. The Salvation Army ARC provided the foundation for Hank to combine work therapy, religious activity, group self-help meetings, and outside medical support for his mood swings. The balanced ARC program was just what Hank needed.

He says, "The ARC provides the foundation for the successful reentry into mainstream society, but only those who put forth individual effort can actually succeed."

The balanced spiritual and social program of the ARC has met Hank's need. Today, he proudly says, "Since completing the ARC program I am now living independently, and I am also gainfully employed, which assists my quest to reach my goal and potential."

MEDITATION: *Strength of purpose is the product of humble listening to wise advice* (Prov. 20:18; 24:5-6).

PRAYER: *I seek Your wise counsel, O Lord. You know what is right and wrong. You know the direction my life should take. Lead me in the path of righteousness.*

"CINDERELLA"

*K*athy says, "I came from a family of six brothers and one sister. I must say I experienced a good and wonderfully happy childhood." Then, at age twelve, Kathy and her siblings suffered the loss of their mother. After that, life became a struggle, and it seemed as though everything went downhill in her life.

She continues, "My brothers went off to the war, and I was left to take care of the house. I was like a perfect orphaned Cinderella, but I enjoyed it for a time. Then, tragedies and deaths followed. I began to lose all hope and confidence in myself. I'm not sure how or why, but I turned to alcohol." It was not Kathy's past that made her an alcoholic, but the misery and despair of her present.

> I am now a real person who believes in myself. I am not alone anymore.

"When all else failed, I turned to The Salvation Army ARC in Pittsburgh." Kathy found more than her own identity. "There I found Jesus Christ, my self-identity, and I realized that He was the answer to all of my problems." When Kathy shared her story with us, she said, "I am now a real person who believes in myself. I am not alone anymore. I have found peace of mind today. I can face tomorrow because He lives. It's just me and my God. Thank you, Salvation Army."

We wanted to include Kathy's story in this book, because after her own conversion and the beginning of her own sobriety, she stayed on with The Salvation Army for more than a dozen years in Pittsburgh, helping, cheering, and encouraging hundreds of others to believe that they, too, could live sober, happy lives in Jesus Christ.

Last year, God called Kathy home to be with Him in eternity. All of us who have been touched by her life say, "Thank you, Kathy."

MEDITATION: *A saintly woman is worth more than any material wealth. A saintly woman cares for the poor. A saintly woman is a good worker. A saintly woman earns everyone's praise* (Prov. 31:10-31).

PRAYER: *Help me, Lord, to appreciate and respect the godly dignity of saintly women, and help me to support the struggle of those who are trying to better themselves in Jesus Christ.*

I ASKED THE
COURT TO LET ME
QUIT THE ARC

There were days when I wanted to give up.

Sam has a loving mother who called The Salvation Army Northern New England Adult Rehabilitation Center in Portland, Maine, looking for her son. The Center staff located him in the county jail.

A long-term cocaine user, Sam had been captured by the police while trying to cover up the evidence of a gang drug deal.

About the early days of recovery Sam says, "There were days when I wanted to give up." He even petitioned the court to leave the Salvation Army program at one point, but later accepted Jesus as his Savior. Finally Sam made a real commitment to his own recovery.

Today, Sam is a successful ARC graduate with thirteen years of sobriety to build on. He completed his GED while at the Center and is now working with his father and attending culinary college.

He returns to the Center every week to lead a twelve-step group for the new men who are trying to change their lives.

MEDITATION: *We are learning to appreciate God's timing and to be aware of the seasons in our own lives* (Eccl. 3:1-8). *We are also learning that an honest day's work brings its own satisfaction* (Eccl. 5:12).

PRAYER: *Teach me, O Lord, how to find satisfaction in washing a car, fixing a bike, and frying an egg. Keep my mind focused on the basics, so I can live life on Your terms.*

LOVE IN
OLD SAN JUAN

*S*ome of us need to re-
cover from alcohol and other drugs. Some of us
need to recover from depression. This is Paul's
story:

"It all started in 1981 when my wife asked me
for a divorce. My son, Michael, was less than a
year old, and my daughter, Ileana, was five. To
put it mildly, I was very upset. My wife moved out
of our apartment with the kids, leaving me alone.
Because of my severe depression, I lost my job
with the General Electric Credit Corp."

Paul came to Puerto Rico in an attempt to visit
his children. For a few months he was able to stay
in his grandmother-in-law's apartment, but
eventually was told that he had to move out.
Since he had no job and no money, he also had
no home. His depression and sense of hopelessness increased.

Then, he says, "Someone suggested that I try
the Salvation Army ARC in San Juan."

Paul came to the ARC, and they were willing to
take him in without asking him too many ques-
tions about his background. Since The Salvation
Army ARC is funded by selling clothing and fur-

niture in its thrift shops, it did not require Paul to have insurance or any income—he didn't even have a specific medical or psychiatric problem.

"When I first came, I lived in a dorm with five other men, and the living conditions were not very good. The heat and mosquitos kept me from sleeping."

However, the officers and staff of the Center continued to love Paul and show him the love of God. In time, he acclimated to the change from mainland living to living in Puerto Rico.

Today he surmises, "My will to survive and overcome my cir-

I attribute my being alive today to God's love for me.

cumstances kept me going. With absolute certainty I attribute my being alive today to God's love for me." Paul found God's love in Old San Juan.

MEDITATION: *Where there is life, there is hope. We know that we are in the hands of God* (Eccl. 9:1-4).

PRAYER: *There is no power, Lord, greater than You. You are the answer to every doubt, every hurt, every depression, and every sin in my life. My hope is in You, Lord.*

GRADUATES
ALWAYS WELCOME

*V*incent had two en-counters with the ARC. He came to the Jersey City ARC as a young adult because he had started to drink and it was destroying his life. It was there that he first found God.

After a year, he left the ARC. He met and married a wonderful woman, and for the next seventeen years, Vincent maintained his sobriety. They had a great life together. Then tragedy struck.

After a year of battling lung cancer, Vincent's wife died.

Vincent says at that point he turned his back on God, family, and friends. "I blamed them for all my hurt.

I went back to the same Salvation Army Center that had helped me 18 years before.

"I started drinking and drugging myself into oblivion. My behavior landed me in jail for nine months.

"When I got out, I went back to the same Salvation Army Center that had helped me eighteen years before. Thank God, they were willing to take me in.

"Although I am not saintly, I do have God back in my life. I consider Jesus Christ to be my friend, and I intend to stay yoked to Him forever. It is no longer I who lives, but Christ who lives in me."

Vincent became a Soldier in the Salvation Army a little more than three years ago. He says he is experiencing peace, joy, love, and happiness since he has reclaimed Jesus Christ as his Savior.

MEDITATION: *Our wives appear wonderful to us. They symbolize the best of everything to us* (Song of Sol. 6:10). *We expect our marriages to be permanent* (Song of Sol. 8:6-7).

PRAYER: *I sorrow over all the relationships and family members I have lost or, regretfully, discarded, Lord. Help me to restore what can be restored, and heal my wounds where no restoration is possible.*

SIX

THEY FOUND JESUS THE SAVIOR

When our minds were confused.
When our drinking buddies were all gone.
When our families had said, "Enough is enough!
When *hope* was a dirty word and personal
cleanliness had become a lost dream.
When the court, or our moms, or our marriage
partners, had told us that we could never see
our kids again.
When our nights were black
and we couldn't see the stars.
When we were sick and tired of being sick
and tired.
Then we found Him: Jesus. And He is real.
And He cares about us.

COCAINE
ROLLER COASTER

*T*ammy was accepted as a member of her local church and baptized on February 9, 1993, but she took the long way to get there.

Tammy came from a family of five and had a rough start. "Mom and Pop separated when I was four years old due to alcohol abuse."

Tammy drank from age thirteen until she turned twenty-five. She entered treatment and was able to stay sober for nine months, but says, "I was not spiritually motivated, so I started smoking cocaine. Coke took me on a roller-coaster ride that left me with almost nothing. I lost respect for myself, my family, and everybody. I spent all my money on coke. It was like chasing a rainbow. . . . I became addicted to cocaine. I'd substituted one addiction for the other, it was awful."

The last Christmas of her addiction, Tammy spent both unemployment checks getting high and says, "I could not stop by myself. I came to the realization that I needed help."

This time, Tammy invited Jesus Christ to be the

Higher Power she so desperately needed: "I didn't know what I was doing anymore, I kept asking why, why?" She cried out to anyone who cared to hear, "I can't live like this!"

Tammy asked God to come into her life and show her another way to live without drinks and drugs. She says, "So He put me in spiritual surroundings, and now I am learning."

She asked God to give her patience and direction and "asked Him to help me understand Him better and bring me closer to Him."

He put me in spiritual surroundings, and now I am learning.

The Salvation Army ARC and Tammy's new, loving church, are both very important to her, but the secret of her success is finding Jesus, the Savior.

MEDITATION: *God's Son, Jesus Christ, prepares our hearts to reveal His glory (Isa. 40:3-5). He understands our sorrows and grief and suffered Himself so we might be healed (Isa. 53:3-6).*

PRAYER: *Please accept my gratitude, O Lord, for all You have done for me. You have forgiven my sins and are healing my wounds. You touch me again and again with Your tender love. Thank you.*

RESCUED FROM AMPHETAMINES

*O*n March 22, 1981, Tom was walking the streets of New York City, addicted to amphetamines and homeless, when he heard a Salvation Army street-preaching service where an ARC graduate named Philip was witnessing about living a transformed life through Jesus Christ.

Tom immediately believed, and six days later he entered the Manhattan ARC, where the first night he was there he was so hungry that he "stole" two baked potatoes left over from the dinner meal. The Salvation Army worker who caught him told him that he could keep the baked potatoes and eat them in the dining room, and she gently reminded him that this was not a place where he had to steal in order to eat!

Tom stayed at the ARC for almost two years and says, "This is where I grew in Christ and learned to be a productive man of God."

Tom was reared in a hardworking, scotch-drinking, immigrant Catholic family in Brooklyn, N. Y. He had a good Roman Catholic school education and served honorably in the U. S. Marine Corps during the Korean conflict. He married his high school sweetheart, Patricia, and earned both a BA and an MA from the City University of New York. He became a graduate of the American Academy of Dramatic Arts.

This is where I grew in Christ and learned to be a productive man of God.

But drugs know no cultural or educational boundaries. Tom got hooked on amphetamines, which brought him down to the point where he says, "I was homeless, helpless, and hopeless. I was a broken man." He continues, "My greatest tragedy was not being aware of the love of God and the power of His blood."

Today, through the power of Jesus Christ, Tom has been sober for almost fourteen years. He has been a professional addictions counselor for ten years, holding his New York State CAC credential. He is also a nationally certified addictions counselor at the highest level. With all of his professional background, he still seeks to have his clients understand that in Jesus Christ is their highest hope.

He rejoices, "To God be the glory. Not through my power but by the grace of God, I am what I am. Thank you Jesus!"

MEDITATION: *In the midst of our worst calamity, God is planning a good future for us. He will hear us when we sincerely pray to Him* (Jer. 29:11-13).

PRAYER: *Lord, hear me when I pray. I believe that You want to give me a future and a hope.*

I HEARD
JESUS SPEAK

Milford had religion "forced down my throat" seven nights a week when he was a kid. He was the son and grandson of ministers, but he rejected everything spiritual at age twelve, began using alcohol, which led to heroin within the next year.

Over the next twenty-seven years, Milford would be arrested forty-eight times. He became a polydrug addict, mixing heroin, cocaine, methadone, and wine. Finally, became so burned out that he could not experience a "high" no matter how he tried. Thoughts of suicide surrounded him.

Referred to The Salvation Army Albany ARC, he began taking a fresh look at the religion of his childhood, studying the Bible and praying by himself. One day, all alone, he heard a voice that he says was Jesus, asking him, "Why won't you serve Me?" Milford tried to respond to the voice and to list all the reasons of his childhood, but he couldn't come up with a good rea-

> **I surrendered to the Love of God, and the Holy Spirit cleansed me.**

133

son to ignore the voice. And so, he says, "I surrendered to the love of God, and the Holy Spirit cleansed me."

Milford is now an active member of a local church in Albany, New York, and has been alcohol and drug free since January 16, 1990. He is now attending Bible college in order to respond to the persistent call of ministry he had been running away from for so many years.

Today he says, "I love Jesus and try to live as Jesus wants me to live. I have no other desire."

MEDITATION: *Sometimes, we feel as though Satan has attacked us and won. We grieve over our losses and no one seems to care. Yet, in the midst of our anguish, we believe and find hope in God's love (Lam.3:16-24).*

PRAYER: *I have come from despair to hope, Lord. I have come from weakness to strength. I need to become even closer to You to maintain the hope and strength I need for my life.*

AWOL
IN OMAHA

*I*n 1978, after eight weeks in the navy, Glen went AWOL. He was not caught by the military police, and he traveled across the country to Omaha, Nebraska.

Glen says that his confusion in joining and running away from the navy came because, "I still did not know who I was when I joined up. I went AWOL because of my lack of confidence in my own life."

Glen's life was not always confused. He says, "Of all the memories I have growing up, the happiest was when I was going to the Mayfair Baptist Church. I remember standing next to my mom and seeing my dad on the platform, helping lead worship."

Although Glen's dad almost became a minister, something happened and his parents quit going to church when Glen was about nine years old. Glen and his sister dropped out of church before he entered high school.

Glen was a shy student in school and, once he was no longer attending church, never had any real friends. He confesses, "I daydreamed a lot; I just didn't have confidence in myself. I had no sense of identity, because Christ was not in my life."

In his teens, Glen tried to find identity by studying evolution, witchcraft, science fiction, and reading pornography. It was with this background that Glen entered the navy and then ran away.

I got to know . . . Jesus again.

When Glen landed in Omaha, he says, "I joined the program at the ARC. I never told anyone at the ARC, or even my parents, that I was AWOL from the navy."

However, he says, "During that time, I was working as a janitor in one of the ARC thrift stores. Through God, I got to know one of the clerks at the store. God used this wonderful Christian person to introduce me to Jesus again."

Several months later, Glen began attending the worship services at The Salvation Army Corps in Omaha. "During that time, through God, my military record was taken care of, and I was reunited with my family."

Glen is a very different person from the shy, timid, confused child and teenager of his past. He says, "Through Jesus Christ I have confidence in myself; I know who I am. While I still have problems in my life, I also have Christ. No matter what life throws at me, I still have Jesus Christ."

MEDITATION: *Our God is in the restoration business* (Ezek. 11:17-20). *Our God wants to make us safe, stable, prosperous, and secure once again* (Ezek. 28:25-26).

PRAYER: *In many small ways, I am still running away from You, Lord. This is wrong! Show me again that Your love is greater and more dependable than any of the illusions that tempt me.*

I FOUND JESUS
AT THE V. A.

Stu's conversion and recovery took place at the Veterans Administration hospital in Bath, New York, in October 1990. He says, "It was there, in a nondenominational chapel, that I finally found peace and contentment. I finally accepted myself for who and what I am. It was in that little chapel that I lost all desire to drink and realized that God had not left me, as I had left Him."

Raised in a good Christian family that attended church faithfully, Stu says, "The only problems I had were the usual ones that most of us have growing up."

Although Stu started drinking casually at age thirteen, he says that he had no sense of being addicted to alcohol until after he went into the navy after high school. In the navy, his drinking went from casual to addictive and followed him through his life until the time of his conversion.

He says, "My drinking cost me my wife and my daughter. Physically, it had caused me to lose 80 percent of my stomach, become a chronic carrier of pancreatitis, and made me a borderline diabetic. I was no longer employable."

Stu stayed at the V.A. hospital in Bath for eighteen months, but he points out, "I knew I could not stay clean alone." In April of 1992, he came to the ARC. "I came here not only to stay sober but also to gain a more spiritual outlook on life."

In the chapel, my problems become very small.

Stu still has problems on a day-to-day basis, but he says, "By spending a few minutes a day in the chapel, my problems become very small, and I feel much more relaxed."

MEDITATION: *When trouble comes, we respond by going to God in prayer. Our God will deliver us* (Dan. 6:10-27).

PRAYER: *You have never ceased to love me and search for me. It is in Your love that I am finally able to accept myself. Thank you, Lord.*

JESUS GAVE ME SELF-RESPECT

*P*eter tells us, "I had a high ol' time in high school! I started to drink when I was only seventeen." He goes on to say, "This addiction continued through my formative years. There were alcohol and drug addictions, trouble with family, the law, and myself—loss of values, friends, freedom, self-respect, religion, pride, self-esteem, health, hygiene, manners, love of life, and love for and of others. I became inwardly focused, full of hate and self-pity."

However, in the midst of his despair, Peter had some good memories, which helped him even then. "I was raised with the religion of Jesus Christ and the power of prayer. Because of my great-grandmother's influence, I learned the Lord's Prayer before I learned the alphabet."

I have found my self-respect and interest in life again.

In 1992, Peter was finally willing to admit that he had hit bottom. A church member encouraged Peter to come to the ARC in Boston. This stranger knew the way he had been before his addictions and wanted to believe that Peter could change back into the person he had been.

Peter remarks, "Since coming to the ARC, I have renewed my belief and love in Jesus Christ as my Savior, believe all my sins are forgiven and forgotten, and I know I have a new life. I'm starting to live as God meant for me to live."

Peter is not interested in "high ol' times" anymore. He says, "I have found my self-respect and interest in life again. I have found that if I give and don't ask in return, things come to me as I need them—this does amaze me! I know I owe all this to Jesus' love for me."

Peter has been sober since June 1992 and adds, "I praise God for all the progress that I am making."

MEDITATION: *Addictions to sex, alcohol, and other drugs create bondages in our lives* (Hosea 4:11-12). *Our God can heal us of all these things. He loves us and wants to take care of us* (Hos. 11:1-4, 8-9).

PRAYER: *Heal me of all addictions, Lord, and destroy all my old idols. All I want is in You.*

TIME BOMB!

*I*f my father was not drunk," recalls Larry, "my brothers and I stayed as far away from him as possible. I was terrified of him. But, if he was drunk, not only could we come out of our room and feel safe, we could sit on his lap and sip his beer or ask for money." Larry explains, "This is where the deception took place in my mind; alcohol seemed to instantly remove the tension from our home."

As he grew up, Larry says, "I carried this demented idea with me; I was like a time bomb waiting to explode." Whenever he looked in the mirror, he saw a duplication of his father: angry, abusive, and quick tempered. Sometimes he wondered whether this was a terrible coincidence, or a tragic consequence.

As a teenager, Larry became addicted to drugs and alcohol and eventually to crack cocaine. According to him, "I was totally out of control and would do anything for my next fix."

Larry began robbing stores and breaking into homes to support his habit. The drugs took away any sense of morality, and he felt no remorse for the crimes he was committing.

But God had a better plan!

On September 9, 1989, five Dayton squad cars surrounded the dope house where Larry was hiding. They found him, and that night he began a fifteen-year prison sentence. He says, "I realized at that point something had to change. The problem was, I didn't yet realize that it was me." During those years, Larry lived in prison in a world of violence and confusion. He was full of anxiety and became suicidal.

Although he was released from prison early, after only three years, he went right back to drugs. Larry says, "This time around, I was completely insane and ended up right back in prison with twelve years left on my original sentence." He says, "I was sure that I would see many sunrises through the cold, hard steel. I was so hurt inside and never wanted to hurt again. One thing was sure: I couldn't beat this problem on my own. I had tried for years and had come up empty handed every time."

And then the miracle happened! "The sixth night I was in jail, I heard a couple of inmates talking about God. The reality of the ever present voice that had been calling me away from the darkness hit me hard. As tears streamed down my anguish-ridden face, I fell to my knees. I looked past the bars and through the window; I begged God to have mercy on me and told Him I would do anything to help Him answer my prayer."

His answer came almost immediately. Another inmate walked over, put his arm around Larry, and told him that he knew exactly how Larry was feeling. He asked Larry if he knew who Jesus Christ was and if he believed in God. Larry continues, "I told him that I had been saved as a young boy, but that I really didn't understand." The other prisoner then led Larry in praying the sinner's prayer. Larry remembers, "I cried like a little child. I joyfully accepted Jesus into my heart and truly knew why I needed Him. I felt so good that night, and we talked about God's love for us and how I could go about loving him back." The prisoner who was ministering to Larry told him that God's gift to us is our life, and what we do with our lives is our gift to Him.

The sixth night I was in jail, I heard a couple of inmates talking about God.

Larry's sense of direction was miraculously transformed, and he began to pray to become a powerful soldier in God's army. He says, "I was miraculously released from prison after that night; God placed me in The Salvation Army ARC."

Larry says, "The ARC counselors were there for me with experience, strength, and hope. It was revealed to me that this is where I could take the time out to strengthen my relationship with God."

Larry became very involved in the worship program and eventually was invited to direct a youth group in the Dayton area. At some point in the future, he also expects to become involved in prison ministry.

Today Larry says, "Through the program, I have gained a strong foundation mentally, physically, and spiritually. God has taken the madness out of my life and replaced it with peace, love, compassion, and, most of all, His Son, Jesus Christ."

MEDITATION: *God wants us to repent and turn to Him so He can restore His Spirit to us* (Joel 2:12-14, 28-29).

PRAYER: *Today, Lord, You are strengthening me mentally, physically, spiritually, and emotionally. You are replacing insanity with sanity. Please continue.*

FROM FAILURE
TO FAITH

*E*ric was the child of alcoholic parents. He could see that his parents' approach to life wasn't working, so, he says, "I always wanted to do things my own way." "I was self-centered and determined to make things work, no matter what the consequences were."

Eric discovered alcohol. "It made me grow up real fast; it was a way of life, but then drinking became a need to help make my life a success." But drinking didn't make Eric a success. He continues, "All that happened was, I became a failure time and time again. I couldn't stop drinking."

Eric's life became increasingly dramatic. He wrecked several cars, tried suicide, and tried running away. Homeless and jobless, he didn't care about himself; all he cared about was his addiction. He continues, "My life was in a shambles. My hopes and dreams had gone out the window." Finally, "I was so empty and tired that I found a detox." The staff at the detox pointed Eric to The Salvation Army ARC in Wilmington, Delaware. Eric was willing to do whatever the ARC staff said, in order to get better.

Then something interesting happened. Eric

decided to believe that God was the One who had led him to shelter. He says, "I started praying and doing everything they required of me. My life started falling into place." For Eric, the decision to give God the credit was carried out in deciding to live a life of service to other people.

Eric has become a responsible, productive person. He says, "I study, pray, and help others, which in return helps me. As the Spirit of God guides me through my problems, I found the success I always wanted: being free

I study, pray, and help others.

from active addiction. I give thanks to my Lord and Savior Jesus Christ."

MEDITATION: *God sees all our manipulations* (Amos 8:4-6), *and yet He wants to restore us and bless those who love Him* (Amos 9:13-15).

PRAYER: *Dear God, I want to be blessed and to be a blessing. I don't want to be one who curses others or is cursed by them. With Your help, I believe change is possible.*

NO LOVE HERE

As a child, Ken never experienced security. With two alcoholic parents, he was often bounced around from one family member to another. Moving in and out of other people's houses and families caused an extra set of difficulties.

I thank God for giving me my life back.

Eventually, Ken became addicted himself. He watched his mother die from a drinking-related illness. Ken thought that was his biggest tragedy. However, it didn't stop his own drinking. He believes, "I had to experience many more struggles before I learned that there is a better way." Ken came to the Jersey City, New Jersey, ARC with desperation in his heart and no- where else to go. The staff at the Center was very important to his recovery.

Ken was able to secure a good job and move into his own apartment on March 5, 1993.

He witnesses, "With my Father sending His only Son to die for me, I praise and thank Him all the time. Now I don't have to drink or drug. I thank God for giving me my life back."

MEDITATION: *God will judge those who have been evil toward us, and restore the damage in our lives* (Obad. 1:10, 17).

PRAYER: *O Lord, I know that You have cared for me, even when I couldn't see You. I do trust You. I believe in You and want to do Your will, today.*

BECAME A REAL MOM WHEN I FOUND JESUS

*V*ictoria was raised in a wealthy Christian home. Her family had high standards, maybe too high. She felt like she couldn't measure up and believed that her parents were disappointed because she was a girl.

She retreated from reality into a world of make believe. Victoria says, "I lived in a world of books and fantasy. I had imaginary friends—animals. I often played alone, pretending to be Nancy Drew or an orphan on a quest for adventure in the woods near my home."

During adolescence, Victoria became rebellious and rejected her parents' religious beliefs. She fell into agnosticism, but this brought her only despair.

She recounts, "Without knowledge of a God, no absolutes, and no basis for right and wrong, I became an existentialist. Drugs went hand in hand with my beliefs. They eased the pain, desperation, and loneliness I felt while living in a world without meaning."

At twenty, she was severely addicted to heroin

and IV cocaine. She spent two months in a rehab center and had two additional months as an outpatient. Soon afterward, she went to Europe where she lived and worked for a year in a Christian community. During her time there, she made a personal decision for Christ and was baptized.

Victoria came back to the U.S., and her recovery went well for five years, but then she relapsed. Back into drugs, she married an addict. The marriage lasted three years before he died from a drug overdose. Shortly after his death, Victoria became pregnant by another man. Still heavily into drugs herself, she sought help through a methadone maintenance program.

Things got better. She comments, "I lived a socially acceptable life. I got into a career I liked, and I did well until my child was seven years old, when I met my current husband."

Again she got pregnant, got married, and had a child. She relapsed into cocaine addiction shortly after her son was born. Within a year, her husband was in jail, and the court had placed her children in protective services.

I trust Him with my life and with the lives of my children.

She pursued her addiction for another year and a half. Finally, the pain of her circumstances drove her back into a rehab program where she spent forty-four days.

From there she was referred to The Salvation

Army ARC for aftercare following her initial rehab.

She says, "It was at the ARC that I recommitted my life to Jesus. I trust Him with my life and with the lives of my children. The Lord speaks to me daily through His Word. He is leading me in His paths of righteousness."

Victoria is facing the future with hope instead of despair. She says, "I pray daily for a willing spirit and for the ability to know God's will and the courage to do it. I live one day at a time, praying for forgiveness for my past and for faith in my future. I am grateful for the opportunity to put my life back together."

MEDITATION: *When we run from God, we bring harm to those around us* (John 1:8), *but when we follow God's directions, others also benefit from our obedience* (Jon. 3:2-3).

PRAYER: *I have failed You many times, Lord, but You have never failed me. When I turned to You, You gave me my life back. Thank you.*

SEVEN

ONE DAY AT A TIME

Members of Alcoholics Anonymous remind each
other that, "alcoholism is a cunning, deceitful,
complex disease," and that it can sneak up on
you at any time, when you least expect it, even
after days or years of recovery. Addiction to
alcohol and other drugs is not easy to break out
of. The genetic factors and other causes of our
addictions don't usually go away immediately,
even when we find Christ as Savior.
We are staying sober for as long as we can, as big
a time period as our newfound faith can believe
for. First, it was minute-by-minute, then
hour-by-hour, and then, wonderful
breakthrough, one day at a time!
Still, we know we are fragile, so we are going to
our meetings and talking to our sponsors
and attending church, and beginning
to say prayers from the heart.
Every day.
For us, like Henry, sobriety is not an option;
it is personal survival. . . .

I TRY TO
BE KIND

My dad was a doctor. Mom stayed home and drank. She was the little secret I had to care for as I grew up."

But Henry had a secret of his own. He says, "I began to drink when I was nine or ten."

"My mother, whom I cared for right until the end, died of cancer before she turned fifty.

"In the 'love '60s,' I was a young adult who took 100 or more trips on LSD. I was not a love child—I was a wreck.

"In the early 1970s, I went through two failed marriages which produced three children.

"During the late 70s and early to mid 80s, I went through several detox/hospitalization episodes and discovered that as a result of my addictions, I have neurological damage. I suffer from short-term memory loss.

"I met God through the ARC. My progress today is ongoing and possible only through God's help. I am on His side now.

> My progress today is ongoing and possible only through God's help.

"I try to be kind, loving, and giving every day. Usually, I stay away from being judgmental—I try to be open-minded and work toward an ideal life."

MEDITATION: *God only asks us to be fair, loving, and humble* (Mic. 6:6-8).

PRAYER: *Lord, I have seen so much hurt and experienced so much grief, that sometimes it is hard for me to believe You really want good things in my life. Still, I will put my hope in You.*

I USED TO LIVE
UNDER THE
10TH STREET BRIDGE

*I*n March of 1986, Thomas went to Camp Ladore on a retreat with the ARC. It was on this retreat that he received Christ in his heart and was born again. However, Thomas says, "Following the Lord wasn't as easy as I thought it would be. On Sundays, I would go to Bible class, and when it was over I would just put my Bible back in the locker. I believed in God, but I just didn't grow in Him."

As a result, in 1988 Thomas relapsed and went back to drinking. After four years of drinking he became so sick that he ended up at Mercy Hospital. From there he returned to the ARC to rebuild his life.

Thomas's life has never been easy. When he was six years old, his father died. Two years after his father's death, his mother remarried. Before the year was out, Thomas's new stepfather died.

Thomas's feelings of anger and abandonment led him to be in constant trouble as a teenager, and he was sent to reform school twice.

While he was in reform school the second time, his mother married again. Thomas got out, but he and the new stepfather did not get along well. He escaped to the bottle at the age of seventeen.

Thomas was married at age twenty. However, he says, "After my wife and I had been married for about a year, we had a terrible fight. I went out and got drunk, stole a car, and got caught and spent two years in prison."

Once out of prison, he started to drink again. He recounts, "I had been to numerous detox centers all over Pittsburgh, but was mostly living under the 10th Street bridge."

I'll continue to grow in the Lord day by day.

Recovery is not always easy, but the program does work if you work it. Thomas came to the ARC in 1992. According to Thomas, "Since my return to the Center, I have been drawn closer to the Lord. I now read the Bible every day. I know the first thirty-nine books of the Bible, and I have read most of the New Testament."

Thomas goes on to say, "I know the Lord is working in my life this time because I have changed. I stopped swearing, and I don't say some of the things I used to."

Thomas's miracle is continuing one day at a time: "I'll continue to grow in the Lord day by day as I pray and talk to Him and He continues to make me a better person."

MEDITATION: *Our God is slow to anger and a refuge in times of trouble* (Nah. 1:3-8).

PRAYER: *Renew a right spirit within me, O Lord. I can control my behavior, but You can restore me in the unseen depths of my soul!*

SLOW AND STEADY
WINS THE RACE

*E*ddie was a big, awkward country boy who moved back in with his domineering father, a two-fisted drinker, after his marriage failed. Eddie followed his father into drink.

I got my father to come to AA with me.

A divorced alcoholic with minor legal problems and a history of drug use, Eddie took forty-two months to complete a normal ninety-day program at the Portland, Maine, ARC. But he made it.

Now the tables were turned. Eddie returned to Vermont as a sober man; he says, "I got my father to come to AA with me, and he also goes to church with me at the Salvation Army Corps."

The roles have reversed in Eddie's life. He is doing well in his own sobriety, and now he is taking care of his father, who has medical complications from his former drinking days.

MEDITATION: *We rejoice in God, in spite of our circumstances. We believe our God will keep us strong, steady and safe* (Hab. 3:17-19).

PRAYER: *I believe in You, Lord, You are my hiding place, my healer, and my strength. You are helping me, and helping my family, too.*

HAVEN'T HAD
A DRINK TODAY

*R*ichard is a man of few words. When asked to give his testimony, he says, "I haven't had a drink today."

Although he was the middle child of a dysfunctional alcoholic family, Richard managed to do well in school, and at first he did well in his career, too. He became a highly paid, successful retail executive. However, the social circle he traveled in included recreational use of alcohol. For his friends, alcohol was just a social lubricant. For Richard, one drink was too many, and a thousand drinks were not enough.

I haven't had a drink today.

He went from a successful retail executive to a street bum. He was in and out of jails, institutions, detoxes, and rehabs more times than he is willing to remember.

When he came to The Salvation Army ARC, he was very careful not to claim any progress that he was not sure of. After ten months in his recovery program, he was suggested for a job with the Salvation Army, which he has held very responsibly.

Still, if you ask Richard whether he will be able to be sober for the rest of his life, he will just tell you, "I haven't had a drink today."

MEDITATION: *We trust in the name of our God. Our God restores us and gives us a name and position* (Zeph. 3:12-20).

PRAYER: *I come to you, Lord, claiming victory only for today. But I know that, as I stay close to You in prayer and obedience, You will give me victory all the remaining days of my life.*

GOD IS
HEALING ME

*U*nfortunately for many people, relapse is part of the recovery process. Bruce says, "My conversion and backslidden condition took place long before entering the ARC. Therefore, my entering the ARC in 1988 was a successful attempt to abstain from alcohol, and my readmittance last year, was, and is, an attempt to find true stability in God."

My abstinence from alcohol cannot, and does not, replace my need for God.

Bruce's childhood and early teens were sad. Because of being rejected by his mother, he was constantly the recipient of some type of abuse.

In 1974, Bruce began using alcohol to fit in with his peer group. He says, "Alcohol enabled me to function, and it allowed me to forget how miserable I was."

His drinking, and the toll it took on him, manifested itself in emotional pain, and he nearly died from pancreatitis.

Bruce is not given to boasting. He states, "My success story is not complete in itself. My returning here proves that something is still missing in my walk with God.

"My abstinence from alcohol cannot, and does not, replace my need for God and for the healing that only He can provide."

MEDITATION: *Our God will bless us, because we have turned to Him* (Hag. 2:19).

PRAYER: *My pain and weakness come from failing to follow You, O Lord. Teach me to stick to Your wise plan for my life, prayer by prayer and day by day.*

ORPHAN-ALCOHOLIC-BIBLE TEACHER

*F*or more than two years Joel has been sober, but he is still cautious. While at the ARC, he said, "This is my fourth time here at The Salvation Army. I hope and pray it will be my last."

When Joel was one year old, his father left. His uncle had his mother committed to a mental hospital and put Joel into an orphans' home. Joel ran away when he was fourteen and went to work when he was fifteen. He worked nights and went to school in the daytime.

Both of Joel's parents died young, both from illnesses related to alcohol.

> I am working a program of daily Bible readings, prayer, and AA meetings.

Joel started drinking with his buddies occasionally while he was in school. Over the years he became a full-fledged alcoholic. Eventually he was convinced by a friend in AA that he should enter detox and a ninety-day program. He entered the ARC and completed the program but relapsed five months later.

Joel's life has had some good periods as well. He says, "I was saved; I accepted Christ as my Savior when I was at the orphans' home. I led a Christian life during my seventeen-year first marriage. I actually taught Sunday school for those years."

Joel knows that the best years of his life were always when he was close to God. His current clean-and-sober life takes this into account: "I have recommitted my life to Christ and am working a program of daily Bible readings, prayer, and AA meetings, and I teach Bible study on Sunday mornings."

MEDITATION: *God rebukes Satan on our behalf and cleanses us from our sin. We give thanks and worship our God* (Zech. 3:1-6; 14:16).

PRAYER: *I claim the blood of Jesus Christ as the answer for all my past sins and the Word as my authority to live a safe and sane, God-fearing life in the future!*

PEACE IS BETTER
THAN CONTROL

*T*he AA Big Book (p. 60) says, "Most people try to live by self-propulsion. Each person is like an actor who wants to run the whole show; is forever trying to arrange the lights, the ballet, the scenery, and the rest of the players in his own way. If his arrangements would only stay put, if only people would do as he wished, the show would be great."

William saw himself as able to manipulate his parents, because they knew nothing about alcoholism and drug abuse. Therefore, William says, "I gravitated toward the crowd that always had the worst reputation; I pretty much manipulated my parents to having my own way."

However, William was not able to control everything in his life. He confesses, "The substances I thought I had control over actually controlled my every breath. Drugs and alcohol had beaten me down, but I was the last to know."

The problems he had before he entered the ARC seemed insurmountable. He says, "It wasn't until, after many attempts, I surrendered to the fact that I was an alcoholic and simply could not drink alcohol that I became teachable again. My success today is due solely to the program of AA and following this simple Twelve-Step Program."

William has had great success since his graduation from the ARC, but he is no longer trying to control everything and everyone around him. He offers, "The material things that I receive today are great, but they don't last forever. It is my peace of mind that I enjoy the most. Every day that I wake up knowing I didn't use the day before is truly a blessing. The best thing about sobriety is being the person I am today and knowing I never have to be the person I was yesterday.

I never have to be the person I was yesterday.

"Today, I consider myself a recovering alcoholic who has a disease called alcoholism. It is a disease I cannot fully recover from, but I can get a daily reprieve, by not taking that first drink, one day, and one day only, at a time."

MEDITATION: *We choose to honor and reverence our God* (Mal. 1:6) *by respecting our friends and co-workers* (Mal. 2:10), *staying faithful to our marriage partners* (Mal. 2:14), *and giving generously to the church* (Mal. 3:8-10).

PRAYER: *Make me a faithful servant, O Lord—with my friends—in my marriage—in my finances. Thank You for all You are doing for me.*

DON'T TAKE
JESUS FOR GRANTED

*B*rian became sober in 1978, but realized there was a huge void in his life. He says, "In 1981, I first received Christ as my Savior," but he continues, "I did not understand the importance of making Him Lord of my life, and by 1985, I became involved in serious sin and soon after relapsed. Divorce followed swiftly."

Brian experienced the loss of those he loved, the loss of a good job, reduced self-esteem, emotional instability, and separation from God, all as a result of his alcoholism and drug addiction.

Yet, with Brian's background, it may not be possible to be sober for any extended period of time unless Jesus Christ becomes the Lord of his life.

Brian came from an alcoholic family and he says, "I always knew that something was not normal, but I still considered my childhood not out of the ordinary."

He grew up disliking his father because of the way his mother and the other children were mistreated through neglect. He vowed never to be like his father.

He says, "My mom tried her best, but could not

cope with my father's drinking. Left to raise four children, she became addicted herself. She died much too young and was very unhappy."

Brian's deep wounds and need for love can only be met by the love of God the Father. He says, "At the ARC, I have begun to completely turn my life over to God. I think I realize better that without Him, I can do nothing; with Him, I can do anything."

Brian is beginning to achieve stability. He says, "After twenty-two months as a client and eighteen months as a live-in employee, I have had a life-changing experience. Although painful at times, I never expected to get what I got here. I am comfortable in my recovery, but I do not take it for granted. I have a wonderful hope for myself, and I know I have been given a great blessing from God."

> **I think I realize better that without Him, I can do nothing.**

MEDITATION: *Jesus cares for all, both those who hurt* (Matt. 5:1-6) *and those who help* (Matt. 5:7-10).

PRAYER: *Heal my wounded spirit, O Lord, with the depth of Your great love for me. Show me how to lead others to You, so that they can also be healed.*

NOT AFRAID
TO SUCCEED

Joe's present stability comes from his realization that, "My successes come daily, hourly, and sometimes minute by minute."

Joe doesn't like to say that he came from a dysfunctional family, but he will admit, "It was not a traditional setting either." His mother divorced when he was a child. The man he thought was his father went to prison. When he was ten years old, his mother also went to prison.

Joe's aunt and her husband adopted him. Later, his mother returned and continued to live with them and had three more children.

Joe recalls, "There was no violence or excessive abuse. In fact, we were loved as best they could love. There was sincere concern, but I believe we all suffered from what is called passive abuse."

With his strange upbringing, it is no wonder that for Joe, "personal, close relationships were always difficult, especially with women. Drug and alcohol use were a major part of my life after leaving home."

Joe's major sense of failure came the day he

went to prison. His biggest success came when he completed his college degree.

However, "A fear of success kept me from achieving any real goals, and I continued substance abuse which eventually led to prison again. One more bout with alcohol and drugs brought me to my knees and to The Salvation Army."

Joe had some early Christian influences, which made it easy for him to reach out to God when he attended classes and services at the ARC. He professes, "The Word of God truly began to have an effect. God has told me that the experience of the Spirit is only the beginning of a wonderful journey—a journey of change, with Christ as the captain of my ship. I am no longer afraid to succeed."

> **The experience of the Spirit is only the beginning of a wonderful journey.**

Not all of Joe's early childhood wounds are completely healed, but he says, "Everytime I recognize a feeling of being less than others, or holier than others, and can turn those feelings over to God, I have succeeded. Everytime I am afraid of what others think and can let go and let God, I am a winner. Everytime I can release feelings of envy and jealousy, with love and sincerity, I know God is working in my life.

"By the grace of God, every time I can be honest, open minded, and willing to change, I have succeeded."

MEDITATION: *God sees our private good deeds and rewards us in public. He hears our private prayers and answers them in public. When we focus on our Provider, He focuses on our provisions* (Matt. 6:4-21).

PRAYER: *Father God, You live in Heaven and Your Name is holy. Your kingdom is coming and Your Will is being done on earth, just as it is in Heaven. Give me what I need today, and forgive me for what I owe You, just as I am forgiving those who owe me. Don't allow me to sin—protect me from Satan. I know You can do this, because the kingdom and power and glory belong to You—always.*

MY WIFE
DIDN'T HAVE
TO TAKE ME BACK

One night, in a blackout, I dreamt someone in a red coat was ministering to me. The next day, I made a few phone calls, and I was taken into The Salvation Army ARC in Southside Pittsburgh."

James had had a normal childhood. He had some success in high school sports, especially softball and football. Married at age twenty-one, he had three sons. Outwardly, his life was going well.

Tragedy struck! James's nine-year marriage ended in divorce, and his ex-wife moved out of town and then out of state with his sons. James lost all contact: "I was devastated and began drinking." He married a second time and had two more sons and acquired a stepson. James says, "I was drunk when we married and was drunk when we were divorced ten years later. Vodka ruled my life, and I lost contact with all family and friends."

In a third try, James began a relationship with an old high school sweetheart, but his drinking slowly destroyed that, too. After many unsuccessful tries at rehabilitation, she told James to get his life together and call her when he finally did. He says, "Months went by, the drinking continued, jobs were lost. The only thing I had was vodka!"

Then came this strange vision which led him to The Salvation Army.

"I had grown away from the Lord and all of the programs and classes were foreign to me. But I decided to listen, and soon I was feeling closer and closer to the Lord. My life began to change. I worked at the desk, drove night trucks, became house manager. The Lord was doing great things in my life."

Things were going so well for James that, after a year of being dry and sober, he gave Sandy a call. She was shocked to hear from him and doubtful that he really had his life together. However, they did meet again, and she liked the changes that had occurred in his life. He says, "We were married on May 20, 1988, in The Salvation Army ARC chapel," where they continued to worship together. After two more years of sobriety, contact was reestablished with James's sons from his first marriage, a wonderful reunion!

Eventually James went to work for another organization, where he maintained his sobriety for two more years. Then he had a back injury, with a great deal of time on his hands, and he says, "I was in trouble—Satan was knocking on my door. I was down and feeling low, and I relapsed after five years of sobriety. It was hard to face myself, let alone my Lord, my family, and The Salvation Army officers; I had let so many people down.

"But . . . they were all behind me, encouraging me to seek the Lord once more. My Savior is always there. I did seek Him, and I feel whole again.

James has regained his sobriety and has come back to work at The Salvation Army, driving the night trucks. He keeps himself "clean" by teaching a Big Book class with the residents in the Center once a week. He says, "My wife and family surround me with love. The love of my Lord, my family, and The Salvation Army has given me strength and encouragement which I am very thankful for."

We were married on May 20, 1988, in The Salvation Army ARC chapel.

MEDITATION: *Jesus heals those who come to Him, rewards our persistent faith, and does not give up until we are fully healed* (Mark 7:25-30).

PRAYER: *Thank you, Lord, for friends and family and Christian teachers who believe in my recovery. Most of all, thank You for Your stubborn love, which never gives up.*

EIGHT

THE POWER OF FAITH

Then we knew people, and we lost them, too.
Then we had opportunities and threw
them away.
Now we can't afford to depend on anything that
doesn't work.
Now we will not believe in anyone that
is not real.
Now we have found that Jesus is real, personal,
caring, and forgiving.
Incredibly, He loves us. And, even more
incredibly, we find ourselves loving Him
in return!
We who had lost all faith are reading the Bible
like it was the morning newspaper!
We are singing in church, like part of the choir!
We are letting go and letting God!

WELCOME
TO AMERICA?

*T*he preface to the NA Big Book says, "Through the development of a conscious contact with God, no addict seeking recovery need die without a chance to find a better way of life." Hugo might have died if he had not met the Lord Jesus Christ in January of 1992.

Hugo came to the U.S.A. with high hopes. He was twelve years old and coming to live with his father. Hugo was rudely awakened when he found out his father "had problems with alcohol. After awhile he kicked me out of his apartment. Ever since, I have been working, supporting myself."

In 1979, Hugo graduated from Brandeis High School in New York. Later, he got married, had two sons, and joined the United States Marine Corps.

Those were the good days, but Hugo says, "Later, my family was taken away from me, I started to lose control of my life and ended up in drug abuse."

Yet Hugo rejoices, "Praise God, because through it all, I met my greatest Friend and Savior: Jesus Christ."

Before meeting Jesus, Hugo spent three years

addicted to heroin and ended up in prison in 1988 for second-degree assault with jail time plus five years' probation.

Today he says, "I have been delivered by the grace and compassion of my Lord Jesus, and I am happy and secure because I have been free from drugs for more than a year. I've met and stayed with my Lord Jesus, and now I have eternal hope and a heavenly purpose. One day I will behold Him in all His glory in heaven."

Through it all, I met my greatest Friend and Savior: Jesus Christ.

Hugo no longer focuses on his past life, but says, "The ARC has helped me to grow in discipline, adoration of my Lord, and fellowship with other children of God." He feels that the religious services, Bible classes, and personal counseling in particular have helped him get closer to God.

Another victory Hugo shares is: "I have learned to control my temper and learned to trust people and the Lord Jesus Christ; I also have accomplished the requirements of becoming an Adherent in The Salvation Army. With the guidance of my Lord, I am looking forward to becoming a full-time Soldier for Jesus Christ!"

MEDITATION: *We gain everything back from God when we give up everything to follow Jesus* (Mark l0:29-31).

PRAYER: *Today, Lord, I am looking forward and not backward. I am no longer looking at my sins, but at Your righteousness. Today, I have a future with You.*

AT PEACE
WITH MYSELF

*I*n my twenties I turned my head and my heart away from God. That's when I got into drugs and a whole host of other bad habits. Things got so bad that I lost my wife, my child, my dignity, and even my self-respect. I didn't even attend my own parents' funerals. The only thing I was good at was hurting myself and everyone around me. I wound up sitting alone on a curb with just the clothes on my back and nowhere to go. It was the end of the world as I had known it.

My spiritual life continues to grow stronger.

"How could I have come to this? I wondered. I'd grown up in a normal family with six brothers and sisters. My father was a hard worker. My mom was a good woman and a great mother.

"As a child, I was very happy. I realized-almost too late-that my happy childhood was because my mom and dad had raised us to believe in God and to worship Him.

"Through the grace of God I found The Salvation Army ARC. It was there that I began to get involved with Church services again. I really began to feel at peace with myself, and for the first time in years I felt like I belonged. My spiritual life continues to grow stronger. I can honestly say that I owe my recovery all to God."

MEDITATION: *Mary praised God for her baby, Jesus* (Luke 1:46-55). *John The Baptist was the prophet of Jesus Christ* (Luke 1:76-79). *The shepherds came to see the baby, Jesus* (Luke 2:15-18). *Jesus was even named by an angel* (Luke 2:21).

PRAYER: *Help me, Lord, to remember the truth I was taught about You as a child. Doubt and disbelief have stolen the goodness and joy of your creation away from me. Let me be like a little child again, trusting and loving You.*

I OPENED
MY HEART
TO GOD

*F*red grew up in a time and place where "life was wonderful. Families were close and neighbors were trustworthy and friendly. Everyone seemed to help one another."

Other than his addiction, Fred says, "I've had very few problems. I joined the service at an early age, and they seemed to take care of me. Back then, we believed in God and in our country. Maybe being in two wars made me turn to God for guidance and protection, and for this I will always be grateful."

With God's help I shall succeed.

Before coming to the ARC, Fred did not really see himself as very much of a spiritual person, although he had a general trust in God. He says, "I never was too much into the Bible."

However, being around other spiritual people in the ARC "showed me and taught me that God and the Good Book were always at my beck-and-call."

Fred is back out in the world these days, which, he says, "has some drawbacks, but working hard and getting things done is part of my success.

"I opened my heart to God, and now I know that I am striving for a goal. With God's help I shall succeed."

MEDITATION: *Jesus is active in our recovery. He heals us when we are broken-hearted* (Luke 4:18-19) *and when we are sick* (Luke 4:38-39). *He makes the demons of addiction depart* (Luke 4:36) *and keep silent* (Luke 4:41). *We are grateful for everything he does for us* (Luke 5:25-26).

PRAYER: *I am opening the old scars and wounds of my heart to You, Lord. I am trusting You to heal me and make me pure and whole again. Thank you, Lord.*

GIVEN THE
LAST RITES

*T*om, the youngest of three children, was born into an Irish Catholic family plagued by alcoholism. He says, "We moved around the country a lot, but I had a very happy childhood and made a lot of friends in school and around the neighborhood. Home life was very good, at least it was until I started getting older."

When Tom was thirteen, his grandfather died of alcoholism. Two years later, his father was shot and killed.

"During all of this time, my drinking and drug intake was increasing. I tried to settle down in my early twenties by getting engaged and having a son. Eventually even that responsibility, which I took seriously, could not help me. I was addicted."

He continues, "Eventually, a beautiful relationship came to an end because my life was out of control. I lost everything, and after numerous detox attempts, I ended up at The Salvation Army.

"While I was staying at The Salvation Army, I became very ill due to self-neglect and a bad chemical reaction. I was in critical condition with liver and kidney failure—they gave me about eighteen hours to live. The people in the Center were praying constantly and with great faith; I had already been given the last rites, and the doctors had told my family that I was going to die.

"Miraculously, my organs started functioning again, and I was out of the hospital and on my feet three weeks later."

Today Tom says, "Thanks to the grace of Jesus, my life was spared. All of the prayers were heard, and I was given a second chance at life. My relationship with my family and son is great now. I am looking forward to a long and happy life serving Jesus and being the best I can be."

Miraculously, my organs started functioning again.

MEDITATION: *We believe in Jesus* (John 4:39-41). *We believe the words of Jesus* (John 4:50). *Jesus wants us to ask Him for our healing* (John 5:5-9). *We hear Jesus, believe God, and receive everlasting life* (John 5:24).

PRAYER: *You have spared my life, Lord, so You must have some purpose in keeping me here. Show me Your will, Lord, so that I can help others as You are continuing to help me.*

LEARNING
THE BASICS

*D*ick had attended special education schools all his life. His goals were to be a fireman and play baseball, but he started forfeiting those dreams when, at age fourteen, he became a weekend partier who drank and did drugs. By the time he was eighteen, the substance abuse was no longer just a weekend activity—he was doing them almost every day.

"At the age of twenty-five, I started doing crack and stealing from my friends and my family. The next thing I knew, my mom had no choice but to throw me out of the house. That is when I knew I needed help."

The Lord saved me from trouble.

After his mom threw him out of the house, he came to the ARC for help. That was November of 1989. Dick graduated from the program in the summer of 1991 and says, "They taught me the basics of living like a human being. I learned how to handle my problems without running and escaping to drugs and drinking. When I began going to church every day, the Lord saved me from trouble. Reading the daily-devotion stories in chapel every day helped a lot. Now that I am home, I am reading the Bible daily, and going to work at the ARC also helps a lot."

MEDITATION: *The reason that Jesus can forgive our sins and heal our addictions is that he was crucified in place of our punishment* (John 19:17-19) *and then conquered sin and Satan by rising from the dead* (John 20:14-17). *Our power for recovery comes directly from his death and resurrection.*

PRAYER: *Lord, the more I learn about You, the better I love You. The more I pray to You, the more I want to serve You. Draw me close, O God.*

GOD REPLACED
THAT LONELY FEELING

*T*he second and third steps of the Alcoholics Anonymous program say that we "came to believe that a Power greater than ourselves could restore us to sanity," and that we "made a decision to turn our will and our lives over to the care of God as we understood Him." That recipe for faith has become Joseph's salvation.

He remembers, "I was a happy child with most of my needs met. Both of my parents cared a lot for me, but there was always something missing in my life. I realize now that I found it hard to express my true feelings to others.

"Not being able to express myself well, I started to drink and act out at the age of thirteen.

"I also had a lot of tragedies in my life. My sister was murdered in 1983. My mother died of alcoholism at the age of forty-two. My life was simply falling apart.

"Since I have been at the ARC, God has answered my prayers, and I can also accept the day-to-day problems with a much clearer understanding.

"Realizing that I am truly blessed in so many

192

ways, I can't describe the good feelings that I now have, but I know that I came to believe that a Power greater than myself could bring me peace within myself, and others. Asking God to replace that lonely feeling brought me a warm, content feeling of serenity and love for myself and my fellow man."

I can't describe the good feelings that I now have.

MEDITATION: *Jesus sends the Spirit from the Father to us to guide us daily* (John 16:12-15).

PRAYER: *I don't think I ever really had peace until I found You, Lord. When I come to You in prayer, You are my shelter from the storms of life. I feel protected and refreshed and able to deal with life.*

A CONTENTED AND PRODUCTIVE LIFE

*G*eorge's fifteen-year-old brother hanged himself. Another died from alcoholism at age twenty-eight. George still has one living brother and one living stepbrother.

George was born at home in York, Pennyslvania, in 1951. George describes his childhood as very strict: "I was taught to be a man by the age of ten years. I always believed in God, but I would only call on Him when I was in trouble; then, after I was safe, I would forget about Him."

George continues, "I started drinking alcoholically at the age of twelve. I was already in trouble—missing school, getting fines for underage drinking, etc. Alcohol destroyed two marriages and numerous employment opportunities for me. I also have had several D.W.I.'s." George was involved in two house fires due to his drinking and his health was abused many times over.

However, failure is never final, and George says, "Today, after being at the ARC for fourteen

The most important point is that God loves me.

months, I have truly been saved and have the Lord with me at all times. Today, I not only pray for things, but I give."

George is now living a truly sober, contented, and productive life. He says, "My spirituality has improved greatly; my health is good; I have a job; but the most important point is that God loves me, and I love Him. I trust and believe in Him."

MEDITATION: *Faith in the name of Jesus makes us strong* (Acts 3:16), *and the way we demonstrate our faith makes Christ real to others* (Acts 3:1-10).

PRAYER: *Father God, help me to live a life that witnesses of Your work and faithfulness to me. Thank you for healing me, Jesus.*

AMBASSADOR
FOR CHRIST

*J*ohn grew up during the Great Depression in an intact family with four brothers and sisters and felt no material denial. He says, "Christianity warmed our lives and home. We went to church weekly to present our personal thanks and praise to the Trinity."

John continues, "How well I knew the power of Christ, yet I allowed the rigors of World War II to cast the best of life aside for alcohol."

Then, through attending AA meetings and the love of a lady he later married, John became a dry, non-drinker. He returned to church and God.

But the story is not all roses: "The death of my wife, the loss of personal monies, and the loss of insurance put me in the lap of poverty and great despair. Prayers once again brought divine intervention my way: I was directed to the Utica, New York, ARC in December of 1981. My doubting heart and mind stabilized, my physical challenges were allayed through several surgical procedures, and I realized that God had a work and a plan for my life. Christian love and understanding grew in my soul."

John graduated from the Utica Center and went about putting his life back together.

John has served for many years as a full-time volunteer counselor at the Boston ARC. John describes the Boston Center this way: "The love of Jesus permeates this facility beyond the measures of most minds. It is cherished each day by every fiber of my mind and heart. The Salvation Army extends to me a reason to live, a place to work, but most of all a place to be about God's plan for my life. The Salvation Army terms my volunteer work 'counseling'; I call it being an 'ambassador for Christ.'"

"Retired" from his full-time volunteer ARC service and living in the Boston area, John still comes to the ARC one day each week to lead the Alcoholics Victorious group. He says, "Regardless of your challenges, dear brothers and sisters, never lose sight of the fact that life is worth living, if such is done with Jesus by your side and as your example. In the spirit of Philippians 4:9, our God will supply all your needs, according to His riches, not only in this world, but in glory to Christ Jesus."

Regardless of your challenges, never lose sight of the fact that life is worth living.

MEDITATION: *We seek God daily, as we read the Bible* (Acts 17:10-12), *and we find Him because we are His children* (Acts 17:24-28).

PRAYER: *Thank you, Lord, for making my life worth living. I want to teach Your Word to others, so that they may also find value in themselves through You.*

POLICEMAN, PRIEST,
OR WISE GUY?

*T*ony was raised by loving Italian Catholic parents. He says there were three career paths open to children in his neighborhood: policeman, priest, or wise guy.

Tony chose the priesthood, sensing the call of God in his life from a very early age. He was a master altar boy by fourteen, reciting the entire mass in Latin.

His parents wanted him to marry and give them grandchildren, so they pressured Tony to give up his dream of entering the priesthood.

Tony obliged them and married, giving his parents a beautiful grandson. He enrolled in Hofstra University and even worked full time, but a deep sense of spiritual discontent had already begun to take its toll.

Later, Tony was employed as a research assistant at the world's largest corporation for the manufacturing of environmental control systems for aircraft and spacecraft, but he still felt restless and, as a result, was unrelenting in his drive to succeed.

Next, Tony became a management consultant to Fortune 500 companies, rubbing elbows with the rich and powerful. Even this success was not enough to satisfy his spiritual hunger, so he turned to alcohol, drugs, and material possessions to try to fill the void in his life.

On his way up the corporate ladder (though his life was already crumbling), Tony was recruited by Reuters News Service to work on Wall Street in their banking and brokerage division. It all looked perfect: wife, child, job with Reuters, a BMW—perfect, perfect, perfect. But with the drinks and drugs, it only took a few months for the life Tony had built to crumble and blow away.

In desperation, Tony checked himself into The Salvation Army in Hempstead, New York, with just one plan: to get back to work, back to the big bucks, and back to the high life. He did make it through the program, even though his interest was superficial. But his mental attitude and emotional condition deteriorated over the next three years until he was transferred from New York to his firm's Florida office, where he began drinking constantly and finally quit his job.

Overextended financially, Tony walked the streets of St. Petersburg, Florida, until he drifted into The Salvation Army ARC in St. Petersburg. His feet were swollen and bleeding as he begged to be admitted. The chaplain called him into his office for a counseling session right on the spot. Tony dropped to his knees and cried out to God for help. Quietly and lovingly, Jesus came into his heart as his personal Savior. Tony began to read the Bible and quickly completed a systematic study of the entire Bible.

Today, Tony has found indescribable joy and peace. He gratefully announces, "The huge empty space in my life has been filled with God's love."

The huge empty space in my life has been filled with God's love.

Tony no longer needs alcohol, drugs, or possessions to make each day worth living. He has chosen The Salvation Army as his life's work and is the full-time chaplain at the Adult Rehabilitation Center in Jacksonville, Florida.

MEDITATION: *It's difficult to act spiritual, unless we really surrender daily to the forgiveness and direction of God's spirit* (Rom. 8:1-2). *When we are surrendered, we sense that God is working everything together for our good* (Rom. 8:28-29).

PRAYER: *What a wonderful fellowship I now have with You, Lord. I never knew I could be loved so much!*

JESUS IS
THE SOURCE

*B*ruce is a man with a drive to excel. He came from an upper-middle-class family of four children where "perfect was not good enough."

He summarizes the problem this way: "Neither physical nor emotional love was shown in my home. I sought the love of God through my conversion to Christ in 1972, but after six months, I left Him for the ways of the world."

In 1975, Bruce became addicted to amphetamines while trying to succeed at two full-time jobs. Later, his addiction switched to cocaine, which he used until he came to the ARC in 1991.

> Here I was able to reevaluate my life; I turned myself over to God completely.

He says that he spent, "eighteen years running away from myself and the calling of God, unable to live with the emotional pain of all my failures."

In March of 1991, Bruce quit his job and entered the ARC. He says, "Here I was able to reevaluate my life; I turned myself over to God completely and was granted deliverance from my addiction to cocaine."

Bruce graduated from seminary on December 21, 1994, and plans to stay in full-time ministry. In counseling other men who are trying to beat their addictions, Bruce shares that, "regardless of disappointments, slips, falls, and what you see and what you hear, you have the reassurance of Jesus Christ which will sustain you."

When asked to describe how he feels about Jesus, Bruce replies, in his deep bass voice, "He is the source for all life, all deliverance, and all healing. He is absolutely everything."

MEDITATION: *We believed in the power of God* (1 Cor. 2:5), *so we received the Spirit of God* (1 Cor. 2:12). *Now, we are the temple of God, because the Spirit of God dwells in us* (1 Cor. 3:16). *God has given us the victory, and we are able to be dependable in our Christian work* (1 Cor. 15:57-58).

PRAYER: *Lord, make me fit for Your service. I want to be a help for those who are coming along behind me. Show me how to pray, and study, and reach out in love to draw others to You.*

NINE

THE FAMILY OF GOD

We thought that we needed a greater opportunity to go back to work. We found that what we needed was an opportunity to participate in our own growth in God's family. Some of us thought we needed to learn how to be more independent. Some wanted to be more dependent. We found that in the family of God, we have become interdependent, both giving care and receiving care.

In our addiction, we knew what it was to be desperately alone. In the spirituality of our recovery, we are learning what it means to have real friends, good friends, close friends.

In our addiction, we deserted people and were deserted by people. In the family of God, we are learning that God's children stick together. Cautiously, tentatively, we are exploring a new world of love, trust, and mutual support.

CHANNEL
OF LOVE

*B*eing raised in a Catholic home," says Peter, "I was forced to go to church in my younger years and broke away from church in my teen years."

Peter's experienced early childhood in an alcoholic environment. His mother divorced his father when he was two years old, so Peter was brought up by his grandmother, while his mother worked. When he was twelve, his mother remarried and had two more children. Peter thought he finally had a normal family then, after about ten years of marriage, his mother divorced again.

Peter recalls, "With alcohol in my family at holidays, the younger children were given something to drink. No one thought there was anyting wrong with that. But at the age of eight, I got drunk for the first time at a neighbor's house. Throughout my teens, drinking was a regular thing with me."

Peter continues, "Then on the morning of November 7, 1978, my mother passed away and I lost everything I lived for. So I began drinking heavily and left my half-brother and sister to go and live on my own. Through my drinking, I lost two apartments and countless jobs, which reduced me to living on the streets.

"I was introduced to the ARC in my hometown, through a mental-health center.

I also am there to listen to what the men have to share with me.

"When I came to the ARC, I felt it was where God wanted me. Going to AA meetings and receiving counseling, both from the Center and outside the Center, helped me move closer to God. I went to a special ARC night in New York City, where the Lord took me by the hand and soul to the mercy seat. What a great feeling of relief that was!"

A short time after that, Peter joined the fellowship of The Salvation Army Church by becoming a Soldier in The Salvation Army. He shares, "It makes me feel good to know that I can do all things through God, who strengthens me each and every day of my life."

Peter is not content to simply receive the love of God for himself through The Salvation Army; he wants to be a channel of love to other men who are struggling for sobriety. "The great thing about being an employee and strong in the Lord is that I can always testify to what can be done in a person's life. I also am there to listen to what the men have to share with me. Just being at the Center gives me strength every day.

"I thank God that I am a worthwhile person again, able to work and live a normal life."

MEDITATION: *God comforts us when we are in trouble, so we comfort each other with God's love* (2 Cor. 1:3-5). *We also try to help with each other's material needs* (2 Cor. 8:14-15) *and we know we can help each other with our prayers* (2 Cor. 1:11).

PRAYER: *You are my greatest Counselor, O Lord. Allow me to care for and guide others as You have guided me.*

SALVATION
SOLDIER

*P*aul found Christ as his Savior after living many years as an alcoholic. One Sunday morning, after the Major had preached in the chapel service at the ARC in Dallas, Texas, the invitation was given for anyone who wanted to come forward to kneel and pray a prayer asking Jesus into their heart. Paul says, "I did go forward and received Christ into my heart and life."

He continues, "Before that wonderful experience of conversion, I had nothing to look forward to. I was miserable. I really needed God in my life."

Because of alcohol and Paul's addiction to it, his wife had left him and taken their little daughter with her. The downhill slide was just beginning for Paul.

Next he moved in with a friend and drinking buddy. He says, "On one occasion when we were both drunk and violent, I killed my friend. I was sent to prison and served ten years of my forty-five-year sentence. After my release, I broke parole and was sent back to prison for three more years."

While he was in prison, a Salvation Army officer came to visit and told him about the Bible correspondence courses offered by The Salvation Army. Paul became interested in the Bible and began reading it more and more.

However, when he was released from prison, he started to drink again and ended up at The Salvation Army's detox program in Dallas, spending forty days there before he moved on to The Adult Rehabilitation Center.

After Paul's conversion at the ARC, the chaplain gave him spiritual counseling, help, and encouragement.

I want to one day be helpful to those who are addicted to alcohol and who are in prison.

Today he can say, "I thank God and The Salvation Army for giving me new direction. I have become a Salvation Army Soldier and a member of The Salvation Army Temple Corps in Dallas, Texas. I want to one day be helpful to those who are addicted to alcohol and who are in prison, by giving them counsel and guidance and by working full time in a counseling position.

"I thank God for my salvation and for Jesus Christ!"

MEDITATION: *There are seventeen ugly works of the flesh which pull us down and pull down others with us. But there are also nine beautiful fruits of the Spirit which renew, rebuild, and energize our lives. Since we now live in the Spirit, let us walk in the Spirit* (Gal. 5:19-25).

PRAYER: *I never got so far down that You couldn't find me, Lord. You are taking the ugly clay of my life and shaping me into something beautiful. Your mercy overwhelms and astounds me, Lord. Thank you.*

BACK IN
THE FAMILY
OF GOD

Ken says, "Today and every day, God is on my side. I have rejoined the Baptist church which I belonged to many years ago. I am really grateful that I do feel God's presence in my life, because without Him I am lost."

Ken came from a very poor but stable family. He had seven brothers and sisters. His mother and father were together throughout his childhood, plus he was raised with respect and good manners. Ken says, "My parents did a good job of raising eight children. But a good family background cannot completely protect a person from addiction."

I've received so many wonderful rewards.

Ken reviews, "Crack cocaine took over my life at an early age. I found I was completely powerless over it, and my life became very unmanageable. So, I chose to go into the rehabilitation program at The Salvation Army. I must say it does work, because I am still clean today after twenty-seven months."

213

Ken rejoined the family of God at The Salvation Army and continues in fellowship with other believers at his Baptist church. He thankfully says, "I've received so many wonderful rewards, and I will continue to receive them as long as I do what I need to be doing, keeping in contact with God in everyday living."

MEDITATION: *God gives us redemption and forgiveness. He makes us accepted in the family of God. In Jesus, we are equal with all believers* (Eph. 1: 6-7; 2:19-20).

PRAYER: *You have given me so much, Lord. I would like to give something back to You. I know You do not really need anything, so I will try to love the new people here, just as You loved me.*

TOUCHED BY
THE HOLY SPIRIT

*J*osé loves to be around friends. He started drinking in his mid-twenties after work with his friends. He says, "This habit became progressive and consequently affected my work performance and personal life, as well as my relationship with my family."

José had a good background, being raised in a Christian home with family values and both parents working. He says, "During high school, I worked part time and graduated from high school by the age of seventeen."

José is bilingual, speaking fluent English and Spanish. He attended the InterAmerican University in San Juan for three years.

In 1991, José attended the ARC Holiness Retreat at Ladore Lodge in Pennsylvania. He says, "I was touched by the Holy Spirit; I decided to become an Adherent at the ARC and attended the class teaching me about the history and doctrine of The Salvation Army."

José became involved in all of the aspects of

It is no longer I that live, but Christ that lives in me.

215

the ARC and today is included in the Bible study which the Center chaplain teaches.

José was enrolled as a Soldier of The Salvation Army (he calls it "A Soldier of Christ") and today leads the morning devotions at the Adult Rehabilitation Center. He is also active in the church fellowship at the Hempstead Citadel Corps and quotes Galatians 2:20 NKJV: "It is no longer I that live, but Christ that lives in me."

MEDITATION: *We have experienced the ups and downs, highs and lows of life* (Phil. 4:12). *Today, we know we can do everything we need to do, through Christ, who gives us strength* (Eph. 4:13). *And we know that God will supply all our needs* (Phil. 4:19).

PRAYER: *Let the beauty of Jesus be seen in me—all Your wonderful passion and purity. Refine my nature until Your beauty shines through my soul.*

REAL FRIENDS
AND FAMILY

*C*arlton's father and mother were functional alcoholics who had fifteen children. He says, "After eight years of child abuse I was taken away by the Children's Aid Society and placed in Children's Village School for Boys until I was twelve; then I was returned to my living hell."

Soon after, Carlton started experimenting with drugs and alcohol, although there were long periods of time that he did not use. He did manage to graduate from high school and from RCA Institute.

Carlton got married and fathered four children of his own.

Then his youngest son died from leukemia. As Carlton puts it, "Then my drug and alcohol addiction came right back, and so did the divorce papers."

After his divorce, Carlton found himself alone and addicted to several drugs and alcohol. He says, "Then came the isolation, resentments, dishonesty, fears, anger, jealousy, and suicide attempts." Just when he thought he had hit bottom, he contracted yellow jaundice and hepatitis B. He found out that what he thought were alcoholic blackouts were actually epileptic seizures.

As a child at the Children's Village School, Carlton had attended church every Sunday for a little over three years. He says, "I knew who God was and who Jesus was, but I thought God, Jesus, and religion were just for good people and good families. It seemed as though I wasn't any good and my family wasn't any good, so I felt Christianity was not meant for me."

In April, 1991, Carlton's life took a complete turn. He had recently been released from the hospital. He was standing on the corner with some other fellows, but he was so obviously sick that a friend started talking to him and convincing him that he needed some help. He told Carlton that if he were to come to the ARC, he could find a way to help himself. According to Carlton, "That was the first time I had ever seen a Salvation Army officer. I will never forget the Major and his wife and the hours of prayer and love they shared with me."

I now know how to give love and accept love.

After growing up in a crazy, abusive family, Carlton found a new family. He says, "Through The Salvation Army's ARC and Corps, I have found a new life that I never knew existed. I now know what it is to be free and filled with the Holy Spirit. I now know how to give love and accept love. I now know how to talk to God and to listen to God."

Carlton says, "Today, I have real friends and family to fellowship with at my Corps. I look forward to doing my League of Mercy service program, and I still return to my ARC to let the young men there know that faith in the Holy Scriptures and in God will bring about a change in their lives."

MEDITATION: *We are redeemed, delivered and strengthened by God so we can encourage each other in love* (Col. 1:9-14).

PRAYER: *I leaned on my own strength, Lord, but I was not strong enough. Now, I am leaning on Your everlasting arms and they are capable and strong. I am finally safe and secure. Thank you, Jesus.*

A NEW
SENSE OF FAMILY

Mike attended church as a child, but started drinking with his friends when he was fifteen. When he was seventeen, he got a job working in the meat-packing business, where his drinking "got the better of me."

Mike says, "I would drink from morning to night. I never had a problem with drugs. Whiskey was my number one drug."

Drinking caused Mike to lose his wife and daughter and everything he had. He admits, "I spent three years on the streets after being laid off from my job. It was a living hell for me. I did not care about myself and just lived for the next drink. After giving up my childhood religion, and trying to do it by myself, I was a lost soul."

Somehow, when Mike came to The Salvation Army ARC, they were able to help him see that God loved him. Mike puts it simply, "They brought me back to Jesus Christ."

That is my way of giving back to Jesus.

Today, Mike has become an Adherent in The Salvation Army and attends his local Salvation Army Corps every Sunday. He says, "That is my way of giving back to Jesus the thanks that is due Him."

Mike has found new friends and a new sense of family at the ARC Center and The Salvation Army Corps.

MEDITATION: *Now, God is teaching us to love each other. We are learning to live sane lives. Each day, we choose to be sober and to experience faith, love, hope, and salvation. We are following God in all things* (1 Thess. 4:9-11, 5:16-23).

PRAYER: *Hear my cry, O Lord. Attend to my prayer. Some days the black clouds come back, and I am afraid again. Touch me once more and heal my fear, Jesus. I believe in You.*

I LEFT THE CIRCUS
AND JOINED
THE SALVATION ARMY

*B*ill ran away to join the circus. It sounds like fun, but it wasn't.

Bill was raised in the church, but when he went off to college, drinking and partying quickly replaced church life as an important value in his life.

As an intellectual during those high-flying college years, he found it easy to remark to a crowd, "If there is a God, I hope He strikes me dead right now." Today he counts his blessings as he says, "How glad I am that God chose to ignore the foolishness of that remark, for I eventually found Jesus as my personal Savior."

At the end of Bill's third year in college, his father died. He had to return home to run the family business, which finally closed. He went through other jobs, but after a couple of restless years, he decided to leave home.

Bill joined the life of circus travel, which he describes as "consuming immorality, drinking, and hopelessness." He says that all the time that

222

he was with the circus, he "continued to feel at a loss about life and my future."

God rescued Bill in a quite unusual way. He describes the situation: "While hitchhiking from one town to another, I was picked up by two men in a car. Within minutes, one man pulled a gun and ordered me to leave all my clothes and money in the car. I shed over $500.00 and my clothes and stood on the side of the road with nothing! Not being streetwise at all, I felt as if my world was finished. Little did I know what God had in store for me."

One man pulled a gun and ordered me to leave all my clothes and money in the car.

After three days on the road, sleeping any place he could find and scavenging for food, Bill ended up on the doorsteps of The Salvation Army in Greenville, South Carolina.

He says, "My first meal was two bologna sandwiches and a bowl of pinto beans. Believe me . . . nothing in the world ever tasted better than bologna sandwiches and pinto beans!" The Salvation Army officer and his wife who were in charge of that program reached out to Bill with the love of God. With reverence in his voice he says, "Thanks to the loving care and support of these dear officers, I slowly began to see the truth."

The message the preacher preached on one particular Sunday was, "Are you following the wrong master?" Bill was moved to tears when he returned to his room after the service. He then paid a visit to the officers' quarters, and there in the den, he gave his life to Jesus Christ.

Bill says, "From that moment on, the pieces began to fall into place, and I felt the call to become a Salvation Army officer." In 1973, Bill accomplished that goal and was commissioned to be a Salvation Army officer and married his wife, Mary Ann.

Today, they are reaching out to provide the love of God and a sense of new spiritual family as the Administrator and Director of Special Services of the Washington/Suburban Maryland Adult Rehabilitation Center.

Bill's favorite Scripture verse is, "Where sin abounded, grace did much more abound" (Rom. 5:20 KJV).

MEDITATION: *God loves us, comforts us, and stabilizes us. We let the Lord direct our hearts to love Him and He gives us peace* (2 Thess. 2:13-17).

PRAYER: *When my heart is overcome, Lord, You become the Rock of my strength. I depend on You for everything and You meet all my needs.*

MIRACLES
STILL HAPPENING

*D*avid's family and friends had had enough. Following many years of substance abuse and countless broken promises, David sighs, "They told me I was no longer welcome at home."

Deep in loneliness and rejection, David was walking the streets with tears in his eyes, nowhere to go, and no one to turn to, when someone told him about the Adult Rehabilitation Center.

The ARC is where David's new life began. David says, "I found shelter, food, clothing, prayer, and a lot of love in that place."

When everything fails, Jesus never does!

Not only did David find love from the officers, staff, and residents of the Center, but he began to pray that the Lord would reunite his family.

God head his prayers and brought David's wife and children back to him. He smiles, "On Easter, 1993, my wife and I were enrolled as Senior Soldiers, and two of our children became Jr. Soldiers at The Salvation Army Corps.

David's wife went on to become Director of

Social Services at The Salvation Army Corps, and once he graduated from his ARC program David became the manager of a Salvation Army thrift store.

David says, "I want people to know that miracles are still happening through Jesus. I know that when everything fails, Jesus never does!"

David and his wife have recently started a special Salvation Army New Hope Corps for recovering people and have been commissioned as auxiliary captains in The Salvation Army!

MEDITATION: *We are learning from our spiritual mentors in the faith. No matter how complicated it looks, our recovery always comes back to believing in Jesus* (1 Tim. 3:16).

PRAYER: *O Lord, You created marriage and created families. Help me to be part of Your spiritual family, and help me to rebuild my own natural family, as much as possible.*

THE
RIGHT PLACE

Richard took the "geographic cure" to Florida (twice) and to New York City (once), but neither one of them worked. He remained in his addiction.

Richard was the third of four children. His father was an engineer for B. F. Goodrich and his mother worked for the Post Office. He comments, "My teenage years were very troubling; there were constant fights at home and I didn't seem to fit in at school."

For the most part, Richard was a loner. He began drinking at fourteen to escape, and he ended up in the hospital two years later for an overdose of valium and alcohol.

He still managed to graduate early from high school, and entered the navy four days later. Richard liked the navy and did well in it. He went to electronics school for a year and began repairing shipboard radar systems. Then he was transferred to San Diego to begin attending college and was later transferred to Ohio and given an ROTC scholarship to Ohio State.

But his addiction was beginning to catch up with him. He began to drink daily after he had completed navy boot camp and was disciplined by the navy for possession of marijuana.

In San Diego he was disciplined by the navy for a DWI while on the military base. Then, at Ohio State, he lost his scholarship due to low grades and began getting arrested while intoxicated. Arrested for a first-degree felony, Richard was convicted, sent to jail for ninety days, and placed on probation.

He began attending AA as a condition of probation and stayed sufficiently sober to complete his Bachelor of Science degree, six and a half years after beginning.

Richard struggled: "I wanted sobriety, but I could never quite achieve sobriety, even though I was in and out of AA quite often. I actually was never able to maintain employment for over a year after college."

I prayed to accept Jesus Christ as my personal Savior.

When he came to the ARC in 1990, he was told that the program was spiritually based, and he says, "Immediately I knew I was in the right place for help getting my life back on track." The Center chaplain introduced him to God through individual Bible studies, and Richard remembers vividly, "During a spiritual retreat, I prayed to accept Jesus Christ as my personal Savior."

Richard moved out of the ARC in 1991 and has been sober since that time. He has also found a spiritual fellowship at The Salvation Army Citadel Corps in his community, where he continues special individual Bible studies with the Corps officer there.

Five years into the recovery journey, Richard says, "God has truly given me rebirth in Christ."

MEDITATION: *Our God gives us power, love, and sanity* (2 Tim. 1:17). *We are planning to keep this new faith until the day God takes us home* (2 Tim. 3:14-17).

PRAYER: *Now that I have found You, Lord, I never want to leave You. Hold me close, O God.*

A FATHER'S
LETTER

*A*ddiction is no re-
*specter of persons. Being the child of a minister, or
of a Salvation Army officer, or even, of a Salvation
Army officer serving in the Adult Rehabilitation
Centers, is no protection against the tragedy of
addiction. This tender letter is from a Salvation
Army officer father to a son who was caught up in
alcoholism.*

Dear David:

For over forty years, your mother and I have
served our Lord in the blessed ranks of The Salvation Army. More than half of this service has
been devoted to the suffering humanity addicted
to alcohol and other drug substances.

Why this particular field?

Both of your grandfathers were, as you know,
alcoholics. Your mother's father drank every day
of his life, for over three decades. Again, both
men found Christ, embraced Him, and were
born again—never to take another drink. Where
did these miracles occur? One in a Corps hall, the
other in an Adult Rehabilitation Center.

With an undeniable certainty, God called us to

this avenue of service. There was no alternative; we had to obey.

Upon becoming our National Commander, Commissioner James Osborne challenged us. He said: "I want a Salvation Army whose people are more concerned about service than security, better at accepting responsibility than rewards, and more involved in the ministry than the mechanics."

We went about serving with great fervor. You, your three sisters, and your brother were part of the package. Five children, dedicated to Christ long before birth—surely no insurmountable problems here . . .

You were bright, intelligent, quick to learn, an achiever, and always compassionate to those who were suffering . . . I remember now how you always loved our men and our appointments, the manner in which you always included them in special events, hockey, graduations, concerts, and the list goes on.

You were bright, intelligent, quick to learn, an achiever. . . . You, my son, found Christ and were filled with His Holy Spirit.

How was I ever to know that you would face some of the same afflictions that brought us to our special ministry? Moreover, if I were to know, could I have in some way prevented your suffering?

Jacob also had a son.

"Joseph had a dream, and when he told it to his brothers, they hated him even more . . . but his father kept the saying in mind" (Genesis 37:5, 11 NAS). . . . Mary wasn't the only one to "ponder" about a child. Fathers do, also. Joseph's dreams were of moon and stars and shocks of corns, and his father indulged him. But if he had known that those dreams would only be realized by suffering and pain and heartbreak, would he have allowed Joseph to go on dreaming? Would I?

Without belaboring the events that spiraled you into the misery of alcohol and other drug substances that surely would have taken your life, I often remember the first visit to a decrepit Mississippi jail. After much prayer, your mother and I purposely waited before visiting you, in order for you to detox. Not a very pleasant thing to experience in the best of circumstances, and these were the worst.

A miracle occurred! Just as magnificent as Joseph's visitation. As powerful as the salvation that cleansed both your grandfathers. You, my son, found Christ and were filled with His Holy Spirit.

I know of the burning love you now bear for the men in your Center and your special awareness of those who are out upon the streets, as you serve as chaplain in the Ft. Worth ARC.

I am also aware of the power that comes from God's Soldier when he tells the addicted that he also had the same addictions. That there is a Cure and that His name is Jesus!

Commissioner Osborne also charged: "I want a Salvation Army whose light will so perpetually shine that it will illumine the pathway of millions who seek to rise from being sinners, to become sinners saved by grace."

And so the torch passes on . . .

For this my son was dead, and is alive again; he was lost, and is found.

I love you, David.
Dad

MEDITATION: *We are learning to live lives which bring credit to God. We are becoming role models for those who follow us. We are saying, "no" to sin and "yes" to sobriety, because we are grateful for God's mercy* (Titus 2:9-15).

PRAYER: *O Lord, You transmit blessings from one generation to another, yet You only hold me responsible for my own sins. Surely, goodness and mercy have found me and will be with me for the rest of my life. Thank you.*

TEN

THERE IS A FUTURE

In the middle of a dark railroad tunnel,
the exit looks far away.
In the storm at sea, safety looks almost
impossible.
But when we have passed through the crisis,
we do find light and safety on the other side.
Now we are on the "Other Side" of our
addictions, and God has given us
a bright and happy future.
We are learning to enjoy the "ordinary" things
of life again: The laughter of our children.
Money in our pocket. Being depended on at
work. The taste of good food.
The comfort of prayer.
No, life hasn't become a rose garden,
but it is good.

SIXTEEN YEARS
OF SOBRIETY

*C*an an addicted woman become sober and lead a sane and stable Christian life? Genevieve says "Yes!" She has now been sober for sixteen years.

"I was born and raised in Spanish Harlem," Genevieve tells us, "I had a Christian mother who sent me to Sunday school, but my alcoholic father died at home, and my mother had a nervous breakdown."

Genevieve came out of this difficult situation as a loner. She worked during the day and drank in the evening. She says, "I had sickness, and I was crippled due to the use of alcohol."

This was due to the Christian influence of sisters in sobriety.

Genevieve married early and then was divorced after having one child—a daughter named Ginger.

Genevieve's recovery began at Talbot House in Providence, Rhode Island. She says that she continued to find the "hope, strength, and guidance in recovery" which she needed at The Salvation Army ARC. Genevieve credits her recovery to "the

237

Christian influence of sisters in sobriety, and friends I found there."

Sixteen years of friendship and Christ have helped Genevieve maintain her sobriety. She is currently employed as a clerk at The Salvation Army thrift store in Providence.

MEDITATION: *In prayer, we thank God for each other, we seek to refresh each other's hearts and live as a spiritual family* (Philem. 1:1-7, 16).

PRAYER: *I pray today, Lord, for all the sisters and brothers in the faith who have helped me on the way up. I am grateful for each one. Bless them today, Lord. Encourage them in the good, and protect them from evil. Amen.*

MARRIED
AND WORKING
FULL-TIME

*C*larence says, "My childhood could be best characterized as confusing." Of this there is no doubt, since his father drank alcohol heavily during his youth and eventually died from medical complications due to his drinking.

Over time Clarence ended up homeless, with a criminal record and a dependency on cocaine and heroin.

Clarence's life began to change when he came to the Anaheim Adult Rehabilitation Center. There, he says, "I discovered a personal relationship with God through the AA Twelve-Step Program. The administrator, counselor, and friends helped me overcome my addiction and other problems as well."

The administrator, counselor, and friends helped me overcome my addiction and other problems as well.

Today, Clarence says, "I am married and living

in Orange County, California. I work full time as a customer-service representative, while attending Cypress College part time." He also serves as a volunteer counselor at the ARC from which he graduated.

MEDITATION: *Our faith is real. We are following the examples of the heroes of the faith. The saints in heaven are cheering for us. We can look at Jesus and find new energy and courage for our lives* (Heb. 11:1-40; 12:1-2).

PRAYER: *Sometimes my life still seems so confusing, Lord. Yet when I pray, the confusion drops away and sometimes I even feel like I can rest my tired head on Your strong chest. Please take away all my sin and weakness, my doubt and sorrow, again.*

TICKET TO
A SUCCESSFUL FUTURE

*J*essie is the oldest of three children. He was raised in a broken home and started stealing early in life to seek attention. Part of the time, Jessie's sister and brother lived with his grandparents, and he was very lonely.

He says, "I started smoking and drinking around the seventh grade, so I started getting into trouble at that time."

After high school, Jessie joined the Marine Corps and started using drugs. He says, "I was smoking marijuana and dropping pills in Vietnam."

When Jessie got out of the service in 1970, he started using heroin and used it off and on until 1978, when he began trying to get rehabilitated. His longest period of clean time was five and a half years, but he relapsed in 1986.

I must return the blessing to another resident.

It was six more years before, "I finally could admit to myself that I needed help." In June, 1992, Jessie went to the VA Hospital and from there to the ARC in July.

Jessie says, "Things really started coming together for me at the VA Hospital. I went from there to the ARC because of its Christian Program.

"I learned how to put together my program here, and I got more in touch with God at the ARC. I stopped smoking here, and also I learned what they wanted me to do. I have a lot of respect for the ARC. Without them, I don't know where I'd be now."

Jessie is the proud holder of a new CDL license, and has been blessed with a job at the ARC. "Now," he says, "I must return the blessing to another resident."

MEDITATION: *We are learning to do our faith, not just to talk about it* (James 1:22-25).

PRAYER: *Lord, You give me everything I need when I ask You for it and do my part. When I do the part I can do, You always complete the portion I cannot do!*

EDUCATION, CAREER, AND MARRIAGE

Mary came from a very strict family, and the rules and regulations belittled her sense of self-worth. She got mixed up with the wrong crowd and had a child at sixteen. All of that brings her to say, "My child's father was very abusive to me verbally, physically, and emotionally. I dropped out of school next. So I had no education."

The low self-esteem that opened Mary up to becoming a mother too soon also opened her up to cocaine and heroin. By the time she came to The Salvation Army ARC, she simply wanted life to be over.

Mary says, "When I came to The Salvation Army, I really had no knowledge of God. Through their church services and Bible classes I learned a lot about Jesus and how to love Him with my whole heart. The officer's wife spent a lot of time with me, teaching me how to know God's will.

They never gave up on me, and they loved me no matter what.

"I now know that God loves me and forgave me

for all I've done, and I finally forgave myself. Now I can go on with my life."

Mary has been clean and sober for more than eight years now. She says, "The Salvation Army has changed my life, with the support of all the staff who showed interest in me, especially Captain and his wife. They never gave up on me, and they loved me no matter what."

Since graduating from the Center, Mary has moved to Allentown, Pennyslyvania, with her husband, Daniel, to whom she was married in 1989.

She now has her GED, a steady job, and she says, "My family is together."

MEDITATION: *Our faith and hope are in God, who "opposes the proud and gives grace to the humble." Let us praise Him for caring enough to restore us to Himself* (1 Pet. 5:5-11).

PRAYER: *Thank you, Lord, for all You have restored, are restoring, and will restore in my life. The power of Your love is almost inconceivable, and Your ability to change circumstances is simply astounding!*

SOBER
AND SOLID

*L*eonard is a man who works more than he talks. His sparsely outlined story is the framework for a great miracle.

Leonard summarizes his story by saying, "I had a normal childhood. At the age of eighteen, I started drinking alcohol mildly. Then I entered the U. S. Army at the age of twenty-two, and my drinking increased."

Leonard then drank in excess for more than twenty years, before he finally decided to make a change in his life and came into the Paterson, New Jersey, ARC. Something unexpected happened at Paterson. As Leonard puts it, "Religion came back into my life, something I had lost during my drinking years."

After being a resident at the Paterson ARC for approximately eighteen months, Leonard was offered the employee position of Warehouse Supervisor. He did so well in that position that two years later he became the general supervisor of the whole Center.

Today when you ask Leonard

Religion came back into my life.

how he is doing, he says, "I now have fifteen years of sobriety," and he qoes back to work.

MEDITATION: *The Lord desires us to seek Him always that He might increase the good work He began in us the day we reached out to Him* (2 Pet. 1:5-11).

Faith is the beginning our new lifestyle, but there is more to it. The next step is honesty with ourselves and others. Then we study God's word to increase our knowledge of Him. Next we work on controlling ourselves emotionally, which is a major part of Christian maturity.

Of course we also learn to hold on to God in tough times. Add to that a clean and pure heart— all the way through. . . . Next we work on really loving our friends and family. And how about loving everybody else?

Yes, it could take a lifetime, but that is what our new life is supposed to take, isn't it? (2 Pet. 1:5)

PRAYER: *Lord, I just want to get on with being a Christian. No fancy speeches. No elaborate ceremonies. All I had to say when I first met You was, "Jesus, help me." Today, I'm saying it again.*

TODAY I HAVE A
WONDERFUL FAMILY

I was a twenty-six-year-old pregnant cocaine addict!" says Barbara, "When I first found out I was pregnant, I swore I would never do drugs again."

Unfortunately, that decision didn't last long. Barbara's drug abuse started again, and she proceeded to lose her job, her friends, and her material possessions. She was also endangering her baby's life.

She says, "I knew right from wrong and had come from a very intact loving family in which we were all very close. But knowing right from wrong just wasn't enough this time, because the addiction had taken over my life completely."

After numerous attempts over several months to try and help her, Barbara's parents found the strength to take the one thing that she had left away from her, her son. They decided that they would care for him until she got the help that she needed. That help came from The Salvation Army Women's Recovery Home in Fresno, California.

"With the help of the program and the people involved," says Barbara, "I learned how to re-build my life, to again believe in Jesus Christ instead of blaming Him. I learned to love myself again, and fought very hard to once again become a contributing member of society."

At the Fresno Women's ARC program, Barbara regained the confidence to make the right decisions and stick with them.

"Today," Barbara reports, "I have been clean for nine years. I am married to a wonderful man, and we have four beautiful children. Along with being a wife and mother, I do catering.

I am married to a wonderful man, and we have four beautiful children.

"I love being a Christian and enjoy helping others in the recovery process. My life has been richly blessed. I thank God for my recovery and my second chance."

Looking back, Barbara is very grateful for her parents, for their strength and their courage, and for their not giving up on her even after she had given up on herself, and for loving enough to go to any lengths to save her life and the life of their grandson.

She says, "I thank God for places like The Salvation Army that provide a safe place for women in need. These people had faith in me, they encouraged me, and they saw something in me that I could not see in myself: life! Praise Jesus!"

MEDITATION: *We confessed our sins, and God forgave us. He will continue to forgive us as we seek* to serve Him and walk in the light of His ways (1 John 1:5-10).

PRAYER: *God, I tried to love myself without loving You, but I couldn't make it work. You are the source of my newfound self-worth. Thank you.*

PLEASURE
OUT OF FAILURE

I can recall, very vividly, my first significant encounter with alcohol," John remembers. "I was found, at age fourteen, passed out in the village park by our night watchman. I can only imagine the humiliation my parents had to feel when the news was out that I was incarcerated, the youngest person to ever be arrested for intoxication in my small town in Ohio, and the first person to occupy that cell in well over thirty years. They didn't even have a key to the cell; that in itself tells you how out of place such actions were in that little village."

John believes that he had wonderful parents, but his recollection of his early years is not very clear. He says there is something missing in his memory. In fact, John says, "I spent a lifetime in pretending, rejecting, denying reality, and in godless despair."

Even in the military, John was unable to adapt and spent the last nineteen months of his service in the stockade, receiving a bad-conduct discharge.

In civilian life his conduct led to the reformatory, county jails, city jails, a Columbus work house, and even into hospitals. John inhabited many other jail cells, most of which did have a key but none of which had any effect on his mind-set. As he puts it, "I foolishly spent many, many years traveling the side streets and back roads of life."

As John reasons, "It would seem that I received pleasure from failures—not just mine but everyone's failures. I was a failure as a husband, father, employee, or anything I attempted."

In 1983, John says, "I had reached the point where I had nothing left to destroy; I had polluted my life to the extent that I felt I had become debris. I found myself nearly every night in a drunken stupor on the Broad Street bridge, wanting desperately to find enough courage to jump in the muddy waters rushing by and join myself with the other debris."

On one particular night in April of 1983, John sat on the railing of the bridge for what seemed to him to be hours. He says, "I can recall crying and begging the same God that I turned my back on to give me the strength and courage to put an end to my miserable life." His most vivid memory of that night is that it suddenly began to rain, a hard rain. Sometime after it began raining, John says, "I felt

> I felt strong hands on my arms, pulling me from the rail. I can count the days of missed work in these past ten years on one hand.

251

strong hands on my arms, pulling me from the rail."

The police officer who rescued John was later to tell him that he had seen him sitting on the bridge many times and never gave it any thought. What made him stop that particular night was the rain, when he saw John sitting un-moving in the cold.

Was the rain merely a coincidence, or was it divine intervention in response to his pleas to put an end to his miserable life? "I much prefer to believe in the latter, because He certainly did put an end to my miserable life, but in the way that I least expected," remarks John.

"It was the casual atmosphere provided me in the ARC that made acceptance and change so much easier. I marveled at the lack of pressure to embrace the faith, but they were letting me know in a subtle way how much easier belief could make life."

He continues, "Life is so much simpler since I accepted Jesus Christ as my Savior. Life is such a joy now; each new day is full of promises and hope."

John is now the food-service manager in the Center where his life was saved. He is in his tenth year of sobriety and has recently completed his first year of being smoke free.

After a lifetime of a poor work record, he now proudly states, "I can count the days of missed work in these past ten years on one hand."

He also admonishes, "Christian life is no assurance of wealth, health, or happiness. But it certainly prepares one to face up to and overcome obstacles. With all its hardships and unpleasantness, I never want to forget my past; a brief reflection now and then makes the life I have today even more precious to me. Praise to God, I love Him dearly and hope to serve Him well all my days."

MEDITATION: *We receive grace, mercy, peace, truth, and love from the Father and the Son. We pass these things on to everyone we meet* (2 John 1:3-6).

PRAYER: *In the midst of my despair, You came and found me, O Lord. I have received so much from You. Help me to be strong in the faith, and help me to find others who need You the same way I do.*

I FOUND OUT
HOW TO LIVE

Wilbur's mother died on Christmas Eve, 1958; he was fourteen. That's when he took his first drink and had his first drunk.

Prior to that time he says, "I was raised in a very loving and caring family, the son of a fireman and a loving mother. I was an honor student and led a very happy life until my mother died."

That death was the beginning of an adult life full of the terrors of addiction. Wilbur says, "I used heroin, cocaine, marijuana, and alcohol on a daily basis. Alcohol and drugs took their toll through the years in broken marriages, abandoned children, prison terms, mental institutions, numerous detox and rehabilitation programs—nothing worked. I lived a life of quiet desperation."

The first time Wilbur came to the Providence ARC, he left to go drinking and drugging. The second time, he says, "I only came here to commit suicide, hoping that my death would benefit someone's living. I can't say how or why, but one day in the sorting room, I cried. It was then I knew Jesus did not want me to take my life, but to give it to service in helping others."

Wilbur says, "Recovery can be very frightening. The guidance received from The Salvation Army officers and counselors has helped me to know where my source of strength lies. I found that the abundant life in the Scriptures must be lived, and that means action."

Today, Wilbur pays his bills, has gone to school, and at the age of forty-nine has a new career. He believes, "Life is now worth living. I came to the Center to die, and I found out how to live. Old things have passed away; all things have become new in Jesus Christ."

I came to the Center to die, and I found out how to live.

MEDITATION: *What a difference Jesus Christ has made in our lives! Today, we pray for each other's prosperity and health, we rejoice because we can care for each other, and we follow the good* (3 John 1:2-14)!

PRAYER: *It's amazing! Anything is possible in Jesus Christ! Lord, help me to believe for the new men and women in recovery, who look so hopeless and beaten down by life. If You could change my life, You can change theirs, too!*

STATE-CERTIFIED
ALCOHOL- AND DRUG-ABUSE
COUNSELOR

*T*ypical of an addicted person," says Ron, "I was raised in a dysfunctional home. My father, an alcoholic, deserted us when I was young. When I was eleven, my mother remarried. This man, my stepfather, was a compulsive gambler who physically and emotionally abused our family. My mother's sense of humor was the only thing that kept us going."

After graduating from high school, Ron joined the army and was stationed in Germany. There, he found Christ through an American living in Holland who preached at the army base.

Ron says, "I had the opportunity to travel to his home, and it was in his living room that first night that he opened the Scriptures and led me to Christ."

Ron's friendship with the young preacher grew, and it was he who suggested that Ron attend Bible college, which Ron did after he was discharged. Ron actually graduated and became an associate pastor of a small church. But a few years passed in the ministry and then his old feelings of discouragement developed.

"Before the ministry, I had used alcohol to cover the pain." Says Ron, "I reverted back to that method. Now that I was drinking, guilt and shame possessed me, and I left the ministry.

"Ten years went by, with a lot of heartache and misery. My wife and child died, I lost a business, and many more terrible things happened. My life bottomed out."

Friends took Ron to a Christian rehab in Florida and his life started to turn around. His goal at that time was to become an alcohol- and drug-abuse counselor. Through a friend, he was told of an opportunity at the Dallas ARC to become a counselor. Ron showed up unannounced in Dallas, and his dream quickly faded when the intake counselor told him that the position was not available. . . .

"But," says Ron, "God is faithful, and I stayed in Dallas, where the captain encouraged me to continue my education in the counseling field. I remained in the program, worked in the Center, and earned enough credit hours and work experience to receive my state and national certification as an alcoholism and drug-abuse counselor."

God is faithful, and I stayed in Dallas.

Doors began to open for Ron to work in the counseling department and he became the intake counselor and program coordinator. When the Dallas ARC chaplain transferred to another

Center, the opportunity opened up for Ron to move to that position.

Since that time, Ron has married, "a wonderful Texan lady, who shares my vision and dreams to continue to serve and nurture men who have addictions."

Now, as chaplain of the Dallas ARC, Ron says, "I am fortunate to be at the best place to accomplish this goal, 'Faithful is He who calls you and He also will bring it to pass.' 1 Thess. 5:24."

MEDITATION:*We pray for each other and praise our Lord and Savior who keeps us stable, one day at a time* (Jude 1:20-25).

PRAYER: *O, what great love You had, to seek me and to buy me back from sin with Your sacrifice on the cross. Your love is greater than I could ever imagine. I will praise You.*

DISC JOCKEY
FOR JESUS

*H*oward was born in Greensboro, North Carolina, and raised in Charlotte. He became a professional broadcaster immediately out of service in Korea and was eventually involved as a professional actor, director, producer, and writer for legitimate stage productions, as well as radio and television. He says, "I traveled most of that time from Charlotte to almost every major city in the United States—except Indianapolis.

"While working as a news broadcast anchor in Charlotte in the '60s, I became involved with a local church and was led' to Christ," explains Howard. "For many years after my salvation, I was very active as a Christian: teaching adult Sunday school, leading visitation groups, and eagerly taking part in almost every church activity possible. I was even privately tutored in the entire Bible for slightly more than six years by my pastor. Because of the pressures and public opinion, I allowed Satan to lead me away from the church, but, oddly enough, I became even more active and more successful in my profession."

Over the years, Howard's family went on to be

with the Lord, until the only members left were his mother, his younger brother, and himself. They decided to move to Florida, where they lived for some years until his younger brother, an ardent fishman, was killed in a diving accident. Shortly after that, Howard's mother passed away very suddenly. Howard says, "I could not take the shock and was treated for several months for acute depression and alcoholism at the Veterans Hospital in Miami."

When he was discharged from the hospital, Howard had no home, no family, and no means of support. He became a street person for almost three years. He now realizes, "Strangely, all during this time God was wooing me back to the church. One evening, in a patch of woods just outside of Sarasota, I fell to my knees and cried out to God."

Howard told God he could not live this way any more and he told God that if He would help him, Howard would go anywhere and do anything that God wanted him to do.

As he tells his story, Howard says, "Several weeks later, I was led to Indianapolis, Indiana, a city which I had never visited and where I knew absolutely no one.

He says, "I was immediately directed to The Salvation Army ARC, where I met two of the most spiritually demanding and loving Christians I have ever known, the Major and his wife."

"With the loving-kindness of God and the guidance of the Majors, I went through the ninety-day work-therapy program and was even voted, "Beneficiary of the Month."

Howard became an Adherent of The Salvation Army and is still a member of the church at The Salvation Army Central City Corps in Indianapolis. He also continues to conduct a weekly Bible discussion group for the men at the ARC.

When God knew it was time, He called Howard back into the broadcasting industry, but this time into Christian broadcasting. Howard is the early-morning staff announcer and host of his own radio program of gospel music on WNTS Radio, Indianapolis, Indiana. The program has a huge listenership, and Howard says, "All of it is for His glory and His praise."

I met two of the most spiritually demanding and loving Christians I have ever known.

Howard is also second in command for the radio station staff as acting chief operator. He makes many public appearances and speaks at various churches and civic groups.

Howard says, "I will be doing these things for quite some time, until God calls me to go to some other place and do whatever He wants me to do."

Our names are written in the Lamb's book of life (Rev. 21:27).

MEDITATION: *We are overcomers! Thank God, we are overcomers!* (1 John 5:4-5; Rev. 2:7, 11, 17, 26;

Rev. 3:5,12, 21; Rev. 21:7.) *Satan is defeated.* (Rev. 20:10.)

PRAYER: *Out of my wandering, sorrow, and night, I came to You, Lord. I was only seeking survival, but You gave me so much more! You are a wonderful God, and a wonderful Savior, Jesus—my Lord!*

MY
OWN STORY

Y̲ou have read ninety-nine true stories in this book. Now it is time for you to tell your own personal story.

First, write a paragraph (or two) about your childhood background, in the section below.

Next, describe your life before you came to the ARC, in the next section.

Third, write four or five sentences telling what you found to be most helpful in your experience at the ARC. Put these in the following section.

Finally, write about your life as it is today—your successes, frustrations, problems, hopes, and dreams. Don't forget to share about your experience with Jesus Christ. Put this in the section, "What My Life Is Like Now."

When you have completed this, you will be the 100th story in your own book! Now, choose a title for your own personal story and place it below:

Title:

My Early Childhood and Teen Years:

My Life before I Came to the ARC:

My Own Story

How I Was Helped While at the ARC:

What My Life Is Like Now:

When you have completed your story, record some of your personal favorite Scriptures on the page provided. You may also wish to write a prayer for yourself and other people you care about.

My Favorite Scriptures:

My Prayer:

Special Thanks

We want to say thank you to all of the officers and staff of the 119 Salvation Army Adult Rehabilitation Centers in the U.S.A.

You are not perfect people, and we know it, but you have loved us when no one else cared at all. And we are grateful.

And our special thanks go to all the store managers, bookkeepers, truck drivers, Advisory Council members, and others who keep the money coming in so that this beautiful Christian program can help the next people in line. They need to find Jesus Christ and rejoin society, just as we have done.

Thank you.

The men and women graduates of the ARC